Gilles!

Welcome to Chalone, now that you've been a part of you will never leave.

Best!

CHALONE

A JOURNEY ON
THE WINE FRONTIER

BY
W. PHILIP WOODWARD
&
GREGORY S. WALTER

THE CHALONE WINE FOUNDATION
⮞
CARNEROS PRESS
SONOMA, CALIFORNIA

ISBN 0-9701030-0-X

Published by
Carneros Press
PO Box 2051
Sonoma, CA 95476

Art Direction by Debra Lamfers
Design by Missy Nery

Printed in the United States of America

First Edition

9 8 7 6 5 4 3 2 1

This book is dedicated to Conger Fawcett, Jack Chambers, Mac McQuown, Bill Hambrecht and Jack Niven, whose commitment and enthusiasm were instrumental during the crucial beginning years of Chalone.

But most of all it is dedicated to Dick Graff, because none of this would have happened without him, and to my wife, Diane, who was always there for me when it counted.

W. Philip Woodward
Chairman
The Chalone Wine Group
Napa, California
April 2000

Acknowledgments

Writing this book has been both a joy as well as a source of anxiety. This anxiety had to do with me stepping out from my comfortable role: that of editor, publisher, and cheerleader. This time I was an author as well.

There are many people I'd like to thank for their hard work and great advice. This book would not have come together without their contributions.

First, I'd like to thank my co-author and friend Phil Woodward. Phil and I were a little tentative with each other at first, but it didn't take long for us to click. I thank Phil for enduring hours of questions he probably thought were overkill. He's a man with a vision, great ideas, a friendly manner and sense of humor to go along with them. Phil, it was a pleasure.

My great friend Jim Laube brought Phil and I together, and I appreciate his guidance along the way, but most of all I appreciate our long friendship.

At the Chalone Wine Group, Phil's Executive Assistant Teresa Vandal excelled at being the main expediter between Phil and me. Angela Bortugno and Patty Rojas helped me choose the photography for the book.

Thanks to Jill Hunting for her superb copyediting and the suggestions that made it much better. I want to also mention Kelly Pierce of ProScribe in Napa. Kelly transcribed the many hours of interviews. She's terrific. Historian William Heintz' work laid the groundwork for the early chapters of this book. Thanks to Debra Lamfers and Missy Nery of Lamfers & Associates – you are both truly masters of your craft.

I'm indebted to Michael Earls and Lesley Berglund for sticking with me through this project.

But most of all, I'd like to thank my wife Lisa for her positive spirit, her "let's get it done" attitude when deadlines seemed impossibly tight, and, well, just for being her usual wonderful and lovely self.

Gregory S. Walter
Sonoma, California
April 2000

Foreword

All of us in the United States grow up with a more or less clearly defined picture of the frontier in our minds. It seems remote in time and place, though it is sometimes brought into sharper focus when we watch a movie or a television film about the Wild West. Phil Woodward's and Greg Walter's book about the struggle to establish and expand a California winery is a reminder that frontiers have been conquered in the not-so-wild West in the recent past, with delectable consequences for American wine lovers.

The book you hold in your hands is a gripping one. It is centered on a piece of real estate called the Gavilan benchland, an inhospitable if savagely beautiful area in central California. Grapes were first planted there at the turn of the (last) century, and gifted pioneer winemakers like Philip Togni and Rodney Strong toiled there in the belief that the soil could be made to yield world-class wines.

But it was not until Dick Graff, a Harvard-educated amateur musician, cook, pilot and philosopher, came to this remarkable spot that it bloomed. If not quite an eccentric, I discovered in 20 years of friendship, he was an extremely rugged individualist. An idealist. An odd combination of a wooly-headed dreamer and a practical man who could build things with his hands. Who else could have recruited family and friends to labor for next to nothing, "a thousand miles from nowhere," as one of them termed it, with no telephone, no electricity and almost no water? Graff did, and then he and Woodward, his partner, turned a tiny vineyard into a publicly held corporation.

Through the most productive years of their lives, and through the pages of this book, march a fascinating file of people: Julia Child, the culinary evangelist; Darrell Corti, the Sacramento grocer whom many California foodies consider the most knowledgeable food-and-wine man around; Kermit Lynch, the Berkeley wine merchant; Eric de Rothschild, the French banker and vineyard owner; Bill Hambrecht, venture capitalist to Silicon Valley, and Paul Hawken, the gardening entrepreneur.

In one way or another, each helped to build Chalone, as Graff's and Woodward's vineyard was called, and then the series of vineyards in California and Washington state that they brought under their corporate umbrella. The story gains drama from the search for capital to finance a business that to most bankers seemed like a fantasy and an indulgence. To Graff and Woodward, it was anything but that; it was a search for excellence—a quintessentially American attempt to prove that the New World could produce wine of a quality approaching the Old World's.

They succeeded, particularly with the Pinot Noirs that Graff turned out in the 1970s and 1980s. In my view, those were among the best Burgundian-style reds ever made in California, evidence of what hard work and cool microclimates like Chalone's could produce. People like Robert Mondavi, tough judges, were profoundly impressed with the Chalone wines.

If the story had ended there, with year-on-year successes for the Chalone Wine Group (which came to include, among other labels, Carmenet, Acacia, Edna Valley and Canoe Ridge), the story might be pure Horatio Alger: worthy but a little tiresome. But Dick Graff was a complicated man. Success undercut rather than reinforced his interest. In a wonderfully, unusually frank section of the book, Woodward tells how Graff's interest wandered in the early 1990s and the quality of the wines he was supposed to be making declined. Eventually, the company's board forced him to retire.

Happily, Chalone recovered, financially as well as vinously, though rivals have caught and sometimes surpassed the flagship Pinot Noir. Woodward had the satisfaction of righting the ship, an adventure he describes in these pages; Graff, tragically, was killed in January 1998. His monument, Woodward writes, is not only the Chalone group but also many techniques, including barrel fermentation, which he pioneered in California.

R. W. Apple, Jr.
The New York Times

Contents

PART ONE

❧

The Early Years

1 | *Early Life on the Benchland*

THE AREA THAT WE KNOW TODAY as Chalone Vineyard had many residents and a rich history long before vines were first planted there.

Among the first such inhabitants were coastal Indians. The Indians who lived between San Francisco and Monterey Bay before the Spanish arrived belonged to about 40 small and separate tribes. It's difficult to know for sure, but each tribe probably had an average of 250 people, and, among the 40 tribes, at least eight different languages were spoken.

Despite these dissimilarities, the Spanish called all Indians by the collective name *Costenos*, or people of the coast. The English-speaking settlers who came after the Spaniards did the same, pronouncing the name *Costanoans*.[1]

Either way, the name was hated and resented by the Indians, partly because it was imposed on them, mostly because it implied that they—an estimated 10,000 people divided among many small groups—were members of one large tribe united by language and customs. If they were to be called by an aggregate name, they felt, let it be Ohlone, a word that may have been Miwok for "western people."[2]

But Ohlone was also an implied name—and a misleading one as well. There was no tribe called Ohlone as there was, for example, a Hopi or a Navajo tribe. Rather each of these California tribes had its own name such as Tuibun, Yrgin, Matalan and, up in the Gavilan Range, the Chollen, or Chalone.[3]

Like the other western tribes, the Chalones were a Stone Age people. They hunted with flint- or obsidian-tipped arrows and made their other tools and weapons of stone, bone or wood. They may have woven baskets, but they did not weave cloth or make pottery or use metal. They did not practice agriculture but instead depended for food solely on gathering and hunting. By all accounts, the hunting was good—grizzly bears, elk, deer, antelope, wolves, rabbits, quail and raccoons.[4]

In 1769 Father Junipero Serra of the Franciscan order founded the first of a string of 21 missions in San Diego. By 1770 the Spanish missionaries had worked their way up the Pacific Coast to the San Francisco Bay Area and, in the next 27 years, they established six missions in Ohlone territory. Like the other missions, their purpose was to convert the Indians of the area to Catholicism and to teach them agriculture, weaving, cattle raising, blacksmithing and other skills, as well as the rudiments of European Christian life and morals. As part of their apprenticeship, the Indians were taught to make adobe bricks, which were used to build the missions. They were also taught to cultivate grapes that the monks fermented into wine.[5]

Like all missions, the six in Ohlone territory ran along El Camino Real—The Royal Way or the King's Highway—which today more or less corresponds to U.S. Highway 101.

The mission closest to the Gavilan range, the eastern border of the Salinas Valley, was Nuestra Señora de la Soledad, founded in 1791 near the foot of the Gavilans, and rebuilt in 1805. By then, there were 725 Indians at the mission.[6] Twenty-one years later, an inventory taken at the mission also reported 3,300 heads of cattle, 5,900 sheep, 52 mules and a vineyard.[7]

In 1823, three centuries after the Spanish conquistador Hernando Cortez overthrew the Aztec empire, Mexico overthrew the Spaniards. It declared itself a republic and in 1834 it secularized the missions; they and their lands were now part of the state. Soon, both monks and Indians began to drift from the missions. In August 12, 1835, the Soledad mission still counted 5,000 vines.[8] Six years later, the vineyard was reported abandoned[9] and the mission was in ruins.

The end of mission winemaking was quickly followed by the beginning of commercial winemaking in California. In 1856 Monterey County had 10,000 vines; two years later, it had 50,000 vines.[10] By the mid-1870s, California had planted 43 million vines and was sending wine across the country.[11]

That commercial "wine rush" passed over the quiet, isolated Gavilans. Up on the benchland, bush, manzanita and chaparral—not grapevines—still covered the ground. Deer, mountain lions, rabbits and other animals still roamed. And there was the occasional bandit who hid in the range's rough terrain. One such outlaw was Joaquin Murietta, known as "Three-Fingered Jack," who in April 1850 stole all the horses in the city of Monterey and drove them up to his hideout in the Gavilans. A posse was formed to follow him, but without horses, it went nowhere.[12]

Otherwise, there was little to shake the stillness. Until the 1870s, in fact, there was not even a visible trail leading up to the Gavilans. Grape growing and winemaking were still well in the future.

LUCIEN CHARLES TAMM was born in Paris on November 25, 1869, the son of Jean August and Augusta Josephine Tamm (Von Naselwitz). While he was still a youngster, the family, which by then also included Lucien Charles' younger sister, Jeanne, immigrated to the United States. By the 1870s, the Tamms had settled in San Francisco, and, soon after, they became homesteaders on the Gavilan Range.

The Homestead Act, which Congress passed in 1862, gave 160 acres of unoccupied public land to a homesteader for a nominal fee if he or she had lived on the land for five years. Or, the land could be acquired after only six months by paying $1.25 per acre.

Jean August died in 1886 at the age of 71, and although the family still maintained its primary home in San Francisco, he was buried in the Soledad Community Cemetery.

In 1892 and again in 1898, his widow Augusta filed homestead applications. In March 1892, her son Lucien Charles also filed a homestead application, giving his name as Charles L. Tamm.

Throughout his life, Tamm used variations of his name. While he was legally Lucien Charles, he more often called himself Charles L., and, for a short period, he added "de" before Tamm. The family also added and subtracted Von Naselwitz from its name, seemingly, at will. In her claim of 1892, Charles' mother gave her name as "Augusta Josephine Tamm Von Naselwitz, widow of J. August Tamm Von Naselwitz." In her 1898 claim, she is "August J. T. Von Naselwitz." And on Charles' death certificate, his name is registered as Lucien Charles Tamm, while his father is listed as "August Von Nasolowitz" (sic). Yet, father, mother and son are buried in the Old Section of the Soledad Cemetery under gravestones that read, respectively, Jean A. Tamm, Augusta J. Tamm and L. C. Tamm.

In their 1892 applications, Charles and Augusta claimed adjoining lots in section 12, township 17, south range 6, east of Mount Diablo Meridian. In a deed dated June 10, 1900, Charles—once again calling himself Charles L. Tamm—purchased four more lots in the same section from Catherine Truxler.

The Gavilan benchland was still a wild place, and the trail that lead up to it, Stonewall Canyon Road, was new and rough and narrow, hacked out along the rim of a canyon. But it was the soil of the land that held its wealth and promise. Composed of limestone and calcium carbonate under volcanic deposits left by prehistoric eruptions of the Pinnacles volcano, this soil has a remarkable likeness to the soil of Burgundy in the Tamms' native France.

In France this kind of soil is laid down in rather even strata. However, in California, where millions of years ago the Pacific plate began sliding under the North American plate, trapping marine deposits between them, limestone deposits are highly irregular. As a result, these deposits tend to be found in veins and pockets scattered around an area. Thus it is relatively rare to find these deposits in extensive tracts, such as they are found on the Gavilan benchland.

Jean August was in his 50s when he emigrated from France and in his 60s when he first came to Gavilan. Very likely, he was acquainted with the soils of French wine country. And most likely, it was he or his son Charles who first recognized the potential wealth of the benchland's earth.

What is certain is that Charles was the first person to plant grapes here. According to August Schmidt, a native of the Soledad area, Charles Tamm planted olive trees on one part of his benchland property, on another part east of the olive trees, he planted the benchland's first wine grapes. The vineyard was located on an 80-acre plot near Shirttail Canyon, close to where Highway 146 now runs up to the Pinnacles National Monument.

While Charles Tamm and his vineyard had a strong influence on his benchland neighbors in the years to come, there is no evidence that he ever made wine from his grapes. In fact, he seems to have spent relatively little time in the area.

Tamm taught French in San Francisco in the 1880s, worked at the city's Belgian Consulate first as chancellor and then as vice consul in the 1890s; then acted as secretary at the French Consulate in the early 1900s. Beginning in 1915, he operated a real estate business. During his life, his residence in San Francisco changed from Geary Street to Post Street and, finally, to Bartlett Street, where he lived for the last 50 years of his life.[13]

His sister Jeanne, who had married and moved to London, returned to California after her divorce. For a while, she stayed at the Gavilan property, but, mostly, she and her three children lived in the Soledad area. She too is buried in the family plot, as Jeanne M. Hudson, in the Soledad cemetery as are her children.

Charles Tamm lived to age 90. A year before his death, he married for the first time—his 36-year-old nurse, Peggy Ryan.[14] Tamm died in San Francisco January 27, 1950.

2 | *Chalone's First Stewards*

ABOUT THREE MILES EAST OF THE TAMM PROPERTY was an 80-acre ranch owned by the Lindgren family. In 1912 it was sold to John C. Dyer, a laborer in a lumber mill south of Fresno. Dyer suffered from malaria that was aggravated, he believed, by the heat of the San Joaquin Valley. Thinking a less extreme climate might ease the symptoms, he decided to move to the more temperate Salinas Valley. Once he arrived, however, he bought property not in the valley but on a benchland 1,800 feet above sea level. It was this parcel of land that years later would become Chalone Vineyard.

Dyer moved to the ranch with his wife Nellie and their five children—George, Verna, Clyde, Wilma and John A. For the children, the benchland was a free and wild paradise. For Dyer Sr., life on the benchland was marked by a twice-daily wrangle with the narrow, pitted dirt road along Stonewall Canyon that connected the ranch with Soledad and the valley.

"Each day during the school session," John A. Dyer recalled, "my father had to hitch up the horse and drive the buggy nine miles down that tortuous mountain road and back again. Then, at the end of the day, he had to repeat the round trip. So pretty soon, he rented a house for us in Soledad and we'd spend only spring, summer, Christmas and other holidays at the ranch with him. But any time we could, we'd be there. We loved the place."

The first railroad had reached Soledad by 1872, and for many years after, the town's position at the end of the line ushered in a time of minor prosperity.[15] By 1909, the people of Soledad were talking about opening a bank and building a road to the Pinnacles.[16] Only six years later, Soledad was a bustling little community with a population of 400[17] and "two hotels, a drug store, bank, newspaper, two mercantile stores, doctor, lawyer, dentist and creamery."[18] But the Gavilan benchland had other, more enticing lures for the Dyers.

Game was still plentiful on the benchland, and there were many mornings when a couple of Dyers would go out early with a shotgun and bring back a rabbit or two. On those mornings, John A. remembered, breakfast would be rabbit and dumplings.

"My father raised grain on the ranch. He plowed the fields every spring with a one-horse single-blade plow. Back and forth all day for days. And he kept bees; he won first prize for his sage honey at the 1915 Panama Pacific Exposition in San Francisco. As a kid, I remember going to school with bee bites."

In one of the many ironies that have marked Chalone's history, these early settlers on the land that was to become one of California's most prestigious wineries were strict prohibitionists. "There was a vineyard on the property just west of us [the Tamm property]," Dyer said. "And there were a few grapevines on our property, too, when my father bought the ranch, in an orchard at the bottom of the hill. But those grapes were strictly for eating. Wine was not allowed on our premises."

In 1920 John C. Dyer finally did move his family to the Salinas Valley, and until he could sell his benchland ranch, he rented it to a woman named Nina Rivers.

Years before, in the 19th century, a prospector named Melville established a mining claim in the Pinnacles area. This maze of basalt spires, jumbled boulders, crevices and caves that rose above the Dyer ranch were formed some 23 million years ago when great cracks appeared in the earth's surface, spewing molten lava and splitting gigantic boulders as easily as one would snap a cookie in two and twisting rocks as though they were moist clay. Centuries later, geologists say, major fault lines beneath the surface moved tons of rocks to the Pinnacles, from their original location about 200 miles to the south. Given time and erosion, the distinct landscape of the Pinnacles was created.

A natural wonderland, it includes not only strange rock formations but also a complex mingling of trees—from digger pines and buckeyes to blue oaks and live oaks—wildflowers, birds, small animals, rodents and reptiles. In 1908 President Theodore Roosevelt declared the Pinnacles a national monument, but it was not until 1933 that development of the area began. However, by the early 1920s the Pinnacles had already become a popular tourist attraction.[19] Despite the poor road and rough conditions, people wanted to see this curiosity.

What others saw as a curiosity, Nina Rivers saw as an opportunity. The only road to the Pinnacles was the one up Stonewall Canyon and across the Dyer property. So she rented the Pinnacles from the Melville family and in turn charged admission to people who wanted to see "her Pinnacles." The fee was 25 cents a person. "Good money in those days," John Dyer said.

On May 20, 1921, John and Nellie Dyer sold their 80-acre benchland ranch to five partners, Francis William Silvear, a friend name George Humes and his three brothers, Roy, Thomas, and Robert, for $2,500, each partner paying $500. In the agreement with Dyer, the five partners were given possession of the property defined as "situated in the West half of the northeast quarter of Section 8, in township 17, South of Range 7, M.D.M., County of Monterey." The first installment was paid the day the agreement was signed, and the last payment was paid on May 20, 1923.

A month later, on June 21, 1923, the partners received the deed to the property. Although Roy, the youngest of the five, is the primary name on the legal papers, it was Francis William Silvear, or Will, who became the primary operator of the ranch. And it is with Will Silvear that the history of wine grape growing begins at Chalone.

❧

LIKE JOHN C. DYER, Will Silvear had a health problem—asthma so severe that he had to spend part of his childhood in bed. "Before I met him," his widow Agnes said, "he moved to the Imperial Valley for a while, and he found the desert climate there helped him somewhat. But in all his life, no matter where he was, he never could take a deep breath as you and I can."

While it was not the desert, the high, dry, clean air of the Gavilan benchland suited Will Silvear. He felt better there, he told Agnes, than in the climate around Watsonville, the low-lying community in Santa Cruz County where his family had a farm.

Will Silvear was born October 7, 1889, in Oregon, where his family had gone to work for a short time; he was the only one of the five Silvear children not born in California. When he was one year old, the family moved back to California, where his mother, Frances Peters Silvear, had been born in 1857 and his father, Thomas Silvear, had lived since arriving from the Midwest in 1853 at the age of two. California was home to the Silvears.

On their return, the Silvears first tried farming in Salinas Valley, but they soon moved to Watsonville, where they bought a dairy farm on Lee Road. For part of the year, they drove their cattle across the valley to the Soledad area. That was how Will Silvear first became acquainted with the Gavilan benchland country.

Each spring, after the meager winter rains, this spare, classic chaparral country is sprinkled with green and splashed with wildflowers—poppies and Red Maids, Blue Lupines and Shooting Stars, violets and Owl's Clover, Indian Paintbrush, Skyrockets, Painted Cups and dozens more. One of Will Silvear's many interests was California wildflowers, and the benchland, awash in pink and violet, cream and yellow, rose and white and blue each spring, was a wonderland for him. Later, after he bought the property, he not only collected wildflowers but grew them as well. He was especially successful with Calochortus (Mariposa), a graceful white, yellow and violet tulip-like bulb flower; and Erythronium (Adder's Tongue), also a bulb flower that has nodding six-part yellow, white and violet blossoms. Silvear sold the bulbs and sometimes the blooms to florists in San Francisco.

The benchland property had another lure for Silvear and particularly for his partners: a mine shaft with deposits of Iceland spar, a double refracting transparent calcite used in optical instruments. But while Iceland spar was plentiful on Gavilan—one still finds fragments scattered on the ground around Chalone—it turned out not to be of optical quality, and some decades later the mine was closed.

Will Silvear built a chicken coop on the property and he experimented, and eventually created, a new breed of capon. He named it Chalone after the peak that topped the Gavilan range, patented it and sold it to the California State Polytechnic University at San Luis Obispo, according to his nephew Robert Silvear.

But what is undoubtedly Will Silvear's greatest accomplishment on the benchland came later, when he began to plant vineyards of fine wine grapes. Silvear had no formal training in viticulture, but he had a deep interest in wine and grapes. He recognized the benchland's rare soil before he bought the property, his brother Roy said. And he was inspired to plant grapes in that soil, Agnes noted, by his neighbor to the west— the benchland's viticultural pioneer, Charles Tamm.

In 1928 Silvear enrolled in a night class at Watsonville High School to study Spanish. Among the dozen students in the class was a young woman named Agnes O'Neill. A native of San Francisco, Agnes had studied agriculture at the University of California at Berkeley and had planned to teach agriculture courses in a rural high school. By the time she graduated in 1924, however, her father had moved from San Francisco to a mountain ranch deep in a redwood forest in Watsonville that the family had owned since 1904. He was farming cherries, plums, apricots, pears and apples, and that meant a long season of harvests. He needed help, and Agnes decided to work there with him. "I never did get a chance to teach," she said.

It was while they were both students in the Spanish class that Agnes visited Will Silvear's Gavilan property for the first time. "He invited the class up to see it. He did have a small vineyard then."

Although the Gavilan property began with five partners, it had always been Will Silvear who ran it. Slowly, he bought out his brothers and friend. By 1930, he was the sole owner.

By 1930, he was also married. Like other people in the Watsonville area, the Silvears had switched from dairy farming to lettuce growing in the low peat soil of the area. And 1930 turned out to be a particularly lucrative year for lettuce. "Will's family never really had much money, but that year was good, so we thought we'd better get married. We had our wedding in July at my family's ranch in Watsonville."

After they were married, the Silvears divided their time, living half the year at the O'Neills' mountain ranch while Agnes's father spent a few months in San Francisco, and the other half living on the benchland.

"While we were on Gavilan, we lived in a house that was straight up the driveway near an oak tree. It had one bedroom, a large living room and a medium-sized kitchen. We had to pump water from the well. Long before we were there, a previous owner had put in cisterns to catch water."

"Will never gave the property a name," Agnes continued. "I suggested naming it after a wildflower but, no, he just continued to call it the Soledad place. During the months we stayed at my family's ranch, Will would still have to spend a lot of time in Soledad tending the grapevines. Sometimes I went along. It depended on what my father wanted me to do. We had an agreement that I would take care of the ranch when he and his second wife—my mother had died—were not there. I often helped with the fruit at the Watsonville ranch, but I never helped pick grapes at the Soledad place."

Will Silvear, with the help of his brother Roy, began to plant his wine grapes—notably Pinot Noir, Pinot Blanc, Chardonnay and Chenin Blanc—during Prohibition. The "noble experiment," the Volstead

National Prohibition Act, went into effect in January 1920 following the 18th Amendment of 1919, which established Prohibition. It lasted until its repeal by the 21st Amendment in December 1933. Between 1920 and 1933, it was illegal to produce or sell any commercial alcoholic beverage in the United States.

The Volstead Act did have a few loopholes, however. It allowed home winemakers to produce up to 200 gallons of wine a year, which meant that while wineries could not make commercial wine, they could sell grapes. The Act also allowed wineries to make so-called medicated wine tonics that required no prescription, and to produce sacramental and other religious wines.

Silvear made no wine for himself during these years. Instead, he sold his grapes, mostly to wineries that made sacramental wines as a way to ride out Prohibition. One of those wineries was Wente Bros., about 100 miles to the north in Livermore.

"Will knew and appreciated fine wine," Agnes said, "although, certainly, he did not grow up with it. He became very good friends with Ernest Wente and learned a great deal about wine from him." After Repeal, when Wente returned to commercial winemaking, Will continued to sell grapes to him."

Even then, Will Silvear made no wine on the benchland, nor did he make plans to add a winery there. "He never had the money to build a winery on the Soledad property," Agnes said. "It was all too expensive. So he grew grapes and sold them to other people. He didn't make wine, except once."

Will Silvear filed an application to make wine at his family's farm in Watsonville September 28, 1936, and on October 16 was issued a wine producer's and blender's basic permit. The next year, on September 27 he filed an application for approval of a bonded winery in a two-story frame building on the farm "on Lee Road, 2.3 miles from the P.O. in the city of Watsonville, Santa Cruz County ..."

That year, after selling most of his crop, he hauled a load of grapes down from the benchland to the Watsonville farm and made wine, fermenting and storing it in 31 containers whose capacities ranged from 40 to 52 gallons. His became Bonded Winery No. 4265, and his wine went by the name "Cima."

The name Cima, Agnes explained, is Spanish for the summit of a mountain, a reference to Mount Chalone, which rose 1,000 feet above Silvear's benchland vineyards. The label was designed by Agnes' sister, Alice, an artist.

Barely two years later, on September 29, 1939, a letter to the Alcohol Tax Unit in San Francisco read: "Application is hereby made for cancellation of my winery bond. All wine has been disposed of, and operations of Bonded Winery No. 4265, Watsonville, California, owned and operated by the undersigned discontinued ..." It was signed "Francis W. Silvear, owner, Bonded Winery No. 4265."

Silvear left no reason for closing the Watsonville winery. Agnes said it was because he realized he would never have money to build a winery on the benchland. His brother Roy, however, told a more sinister story. "One morning when Will wasn't there, a man showed up at our Watsonville winery and said, 'If you put any of this stuff on the market, you won't live.' We all believed he was from one of the big wineries. When I told Will about the threat, he took 15 barrels of wine we had and hid them up there on Soledad property, under the barn, covered with hay. What he ever done with them, I don't know."

Will Silvear never again made wine. But still, his grapes were made into some of California's finest wines of the time. In 1938, he met the man who would become one of the state's greatest winemakers. André Tchelistcheff came to Napa Valley that year as the winemaker of Beaulieu Vineyard and remained there for 35 harvests. Born in Russia, educated in Czechoslovakia and at the Institut Pasteur in Paris, Tchelistcheff was a research enologist at the *Institut National Agronomique* in Paris when Georges de Latour, the founder of Beaulieu, asked him to come to Napa.

"I met Will Silvear soon after I began at Beaulieu," Tchelistcheff remembered. "He was a Francophile to the point that he was acting as a

Frenchman rather than an American man. He admired very probably French Burgundies more than anything else. It was one of the reasons he was so close to Georges de Latour. As a matter of fact, it was de Latour who established this contact before I came to Beaulieu. After I arrived, I simply followed the contact."

"Will Silvear was a big man, a tall man, and he would never simply shake hands; he always grabbed me in his arms," said Tchelistcheff, a neat and trim man of slight build. "He would come to Beaulieu, and there would be a wonderful lunch or dinner before business was discussed. We had interesting tastings together. But price was always a problem. He would say, 'But Mr. de Latour, there is only one fruit that exists in the whole United States of America. That's my Pinot Noir.' You see, he was so proud of it. Georges de Latour, being a very talented businessman, knew how to approach grape growers. He would become very critical and then mellow to almost a sweet honey. So, in those days, the late 1930s, de Latour bought Silvear's Pinot Noir at $18 to $20 a ton. That was at a time when the juice of some lesser grapes was selling for 12 cents to 14 cents a gallon."

Georges de Latour's dream, Tchelistcheff said, was to produce fine quality Burgundy, and to fulfill that dream he needed the proper selection of Pinot Noir stock. According to Tchelistcheff, Beaulieu's Pinot Noir plantings came from two different selections. The first, planted in the late 1890s or early 1900s, came from the old Paul Masson selection. "Paul Masson was actually the original source of Pinot Noir plantation in California," he said.

In the late 1920s or early 1930s, de Latour planted a new block of Pinot Noir, Tchelistcheff said, "at Ranch Number One in Rutherford. That vineyard was more or less the answer to my dreams to make a good Burgundy."

There are two theories about the origins of the stock planted in this second Pinot Noir vineyard. One is that, like the first, the new vineyard was also from Paul Masson stock. A stronger possibility is that it came from Silvear. Those involved in the planting—more than 60 years ago, perhaps longer—are dead, but if one considers Georges de Latour's passionate interest in Silvear's grapes and his willingness to pay Silvear the highest price for those grapes, there is good reason to accept the second theory.

"Silvear also grew Chardonnay," Tchelistcheff noted, "but de Latour was not interested in Chardonnay. As a matter of fact, there was no Chardonnay at Beaulieu at that time. We bought only Pinot Noir from Silvear. Each year he made one delivery to us—never more than 10 tons and usually just about six tons of grapes in wooden boxes. Only a very limited section of his Pinot Noir was coming to Beaulieu."

Georges de Latour, Will Silvear and André Tchelistcheff met together for three vintages to talk about Silvear's grapes and the price de Latour would pay for them. After de Latour's death in 1940, Tchelistcheff dealt directly with Silvear for a few more years. And then the deliveries stopped.

By that time, Silvear was selling a portion of his grapes to Olivier Goulet of Almaden. Goulet had been Brother Olivier Goulet at the Jesuit Fathers' Novitiate of Los Gatos and the novitiate's winemaker until he left both the order and the job in 1936. Soon after, he married and began making wine for Martin Ray, a realtor who had bought the old Paul Masson winery in Los Gatos. In the early 1940s, after he and Ray had a disagreement, Goulet left Masson and went to work for Almaden.

"Olivier was very interested in Will's grapes, especially his Chardonnay and Pinot Noir," Agnes said. "They are the grapes of Champagne, and Olivier wanted to make sparkling wine from them. And for a few years, he did."

Most of the grapes Goulet bought from Silvear were used to make sparkling wine under the Almaden label. But the company also allowed Goulet to make a separate batch that was bottled for Silvear under his own label, "Soledad."

Silvear brought his "Soledad" sparkling wine to the benchland. Earl Mathiesen, whose father owned property bordering the Silvear ranch, recalled visiting the caves where, about 20 years earlier, Silvear and his partners had mined for Iceland spar. In the 1940s, Mathiesen said, "the caves were lined with Champagne bottles."

The wine, in a traditional Champagne bottle, bore a green and white label that read:

F.W. SILVEAR
Soledad
Prepared and bottled by
O.J. Goulet Vineyards
Los Gatos, California

The neck label read:
Pinot Chardonnay
Brut
Naturally Fermented in bottle
Made by the original methode champenoise

There is no vintage date. Like the Cima label, the Soledad label was designed by Agnes's sister, Alice. It featured a drawing of a Champagne glass and grapes with a miniature Champagne glass on each grape.

The rest of Silvear's grapes were sold to Wente and, once, in the mid-1940s, to Mirassou. By then, Will Silvear had doubled his acreage by buying an 80-acre parcel of land from the Gummow family in 1946. The land was contiguous with the original ranch, lying down the slope toward the valley; it later became known as the lower vineyard.

Soon after Goulet made "Soledad," Will and Agnes obtained a license to sell wine in a shop in Freedom, a small town near Watsonville. "At first we sold just wine and beer in our retail store," Agnes said. "We sold not only our wine but everyone's wine. Will made a specialty of fine wines. Then he enlarged the store and got a complete liquor license so we could sell spirits as well."

"We named our store Whiskey Hill Liquors because Whiskey Hill was the old name of Freedom. When I was a child, there were no saloons in Watsonville; it was dry. So all around Watsonville, there were small towns with names like Whiskey Hill and Five Mile House. I ran the store while Will farmed and did all the other things."

Will's "other things" added up to a formidable list. On the benchland there were his vineyards that were his first love and received his greatest dedication. There were also his experiments with chickens and the development of his new breed of capon. And there was his wildflower business. Agnes and Will also had horses that they kept on the benchland in winter "because it was drier and better for their feet," she said. At the O'Neill family ranch, there were fruits to tend. At the Silvear family farm, both lettuce and sugar beets now grew; Will and his brothers had inherited the farm when their father died. And every year at Christmas, Will Silvear added two seasonal ventures. One was his Christmas tree business, for which he would search out the best fir trees in the state and then sell them in a store he rented each December.

The other venture, also based in his December store, was selling Christmas wreaths. "All the years I knew him," Agnes recounted, "he made the most beautiful wreaths anyone ever made; he made them out of redwood. They were not at all like the common ones you see. Each was made of different textures of redwood—for example, the finer-texture wood of the branches and the flatter wood where the cone grows. He made wreaths of holly, too, and they were very beautiful. But he was most famous for his redwood wreaths."

The O'Neill family ranch was surrounded by redwoods, and, each year, Will Silvear would climb these giant redwoods to harvest his wreath material. About 7:30 on a Sunday morning, December 4, 1955, Will went out into the redwood forest with a ladder and a saw. Agnes left lunch for him before going to town; when she returned, it had not been eaten. By 11 p.m., when he had still not returned, she called the sheriff's office. A group of sheriff's deputies and neighbors went out to search for him. They found him two hours later, lying under a redwood tree about 200 yards from the house, dead. The coroner found he had broken several bones and ruptured his aorta in a fall from the tree. After a private service, he was buried in Watsonville. He was 67 years old. He and Agnes had

had no children.

For about a year, Agnes continued to run their wine and liquor store. By then, she said, "I was happy to sell that license to someone else."

After Will's death, she hired a man from Watsonville to take care of the benchland property. When he, too, died less than a year later, she said, "I just couldn't manage it; it was too much."

She put the property up for sale and, in early 1957, sold it to two men from San Francisco: Dr. Edward Liska, a psychiatrist, and John Sigman, a stockbroker. Under their ownership, a new era of winemaking was about to begin.

3 | *Liska, Sigman and Togni*

EDWARD LISKA AND JOHN SIGMAN met almost by chance. Liska, who was born in Connecticut, moved to California in 1947 and began his psychiatric practice in San Francisco five years later; his office was on Buckingham Way. John Sigman, about two years younger than Liska, was a native of Illinois who lived in San Francisco; he worked as a stockbroker for Reynolds & Co., which had a branch office in the same building.

Liska met Sigman when he stopped in the Reynolds branch office one day. Soon, Sigman became Liska's broker, and the two began to meet for lunch to talk about investments and securities.

In early 1957, John Sigman (who was usually called Jack) told Liska about a different kind of investment—a property in the mountain range along the eastern border of Monterey County. The following weekend, the two men drove down to look at it.

The austere beauty, the silence, the space awed them. "I wasn't interested in wine," Liska said, "but the place was wonderful, and I thought it would be great to be able to go there on weekends."

On February 17, 1957, he and Sigman signed a deed of trust for the Silvear benchland property for $12,500. The title was conveyed to them 15 months later, on May 25, 1958 when the payments were completed.

Agnes Silvear had listed the property with a real estate firm, and she and the new owners of Will's Soledad place never met. "They corresponded with me after they bought it," she remembered. "In fact, they wanted me to be their bookkeeper. Isn't that ridiculous? Of course, I declined." Agnes lived on in the log cabin on the O'Neill mountain ranch, surrounded by redwoods. For a while, she managed the ranch's fruit orchards.

The first time Ed Liska returned to the benchland after he and Sigman bought it was March 3, 1957. "There were four buildings on it then—an old house that was virtually uninhabitable, a huge barn that was falling apart, a chicken coop and a small shed. The old house was torn down because it was beyond repair. We purchased an army surplus prefab made primarily of metal, and we dragged it up there. It was like putting a giant erector set together."

Liska would drive down to the benchland on Friday evenings. "I'd work all day Saturday and drive back either that night or on Sunday morning. Sometimes my wife and children would go with me. They would stay at the motel while I worked on the house on the benchland. There was no electrical power up there so it was all grueling manual labor. But I had fun. I like working with my hands."

Philip Togni, who would become Chalone's first winemaker, remembers Liska's hard work. "I was impressed with him. His grandfather had been a carpenter in Poland, and so Liska had his own box of tools, and nothing seemed to suit him better than spending the weekend chiseling away at something. He had these funny little ways. I remember once he and I drove down to Chalone in Sigman's convertible with the top down and had gotten blown around. As soon as we got to the benchland—the moment the car came to a halt—Liska jumped right out with his box of tools, ran up to the house and started working away."

After finishing the rudiments of the main house, he began work on a smaller house that was later called the little house, or caretaker's house.

After a time, though, as much as he enjoyed the work, it seemed to Ed Liska that he was doing most of it. He kept a record of the number of days each of the partners spent at Chalone:

YEAR	LISKA	SIGMAN
1957	19	13
1958	36	32
1959	30	14
1960	27	No record

Soon after they bought the property, the partners realized that even if both had been able to be at the benchland every weekend, it still would not have been enough. There were also the vineyards to tend. So shortly after they bought the Silvear place, Liska and Sigman hired Jack Armbrister to look after the property. A short, wizened man who was also called "Tokay Jack," Armbrister was known to take a long break each afternoon. "I'm going to kiss Mama," he would say and disappear with a bottle of Tokay. Armbrister was a bit difficult and, more often than not, a bit drunk. Still, he helped bring in the first harvest of grapes under the new owners, which was sold to Mirassou Vineyards in San Jose.

It was not an easy harvest. Deer love grapes and they got their fill on the benchland that year. When Armbrister shot one and cut it open, he and Liska found its stomach filled with Pinot Noir and Chardonnay. Another major problem was the lack of water, a consistent problem in the years to come. "There was a well but it had only surface water," Liska said. "Sigman and I had to haul water up in five-gallon tanks. Water was so scarce on the benchland that he and I would rarely drink any when we were up there."

It was soon apparent that the partners needed to put more money into the property. "We decided we'd match dollar for dollar," Liska said, "and we agreed to alternate in keeping the books. So in 1957 I kept them and I paid the bills. In 1958 it was Sigman's turn; in 1959, it was my turn; in 1960, it was Sigman again. Expenses included Armbrister's salary, fertilizer, spray guns and so on. We were to match expenses so that if we owed, let's say, $300, we'd each pay $150. When I kept the books, I realized Jack wasn't putting money in at the same time I was. By 1958 I began to get an idea of Jack's bookkeeping habits."

In 1957 the partnership between Liska and Sigman was named El Venido, although that was not exactly the name they had in mind. What they wanted was El Vinedo—vineyard in Spanish—but when Liska's wife, Claire, went to the bank to open an account under El Vinedo, a clerk misspelled it, and the checkbook was issued to El Venido. For the next three years, Liska and Sigman sold their grapes under the name El Venido.

Then in 1960, Philip Togni entered the scene. He was a winemaker with fine credentials, and Liska was impressed.

"Philip was a young man looking for an opportunity to put his skills to work, and he wanted to be our winemaker. But that required money, and Sigman and I had none. So we decided to become a corporation. We made up an amateurish booklet—pictures, predictive statements. According to Togni, we needed $100,000 for equipment, logo, winery, increased plantings, presses, barrels and so on. But our efforts to raise $100,000 failed; we raised only about $25,000. Still Togni was committed to the idea of making wine here. It was the beginning of the wine explosion in California. So despite poor capitalization, we reached an understanding with Togni and decided to go ahead." In March 1960 Philip Togni began to work for Liska & Sigman.

As Edward Liska remembers it, "Part of our agreement was that Togni would be given some shares. I must admit, I've never been much of a businessman."

As Philip Togni remembers it, "Sigman and Liska said, 'Take charge.' They would pay a salary; also, they were going to divide 25 acres into five-acre pieces, and I was to get one of the pieces. I marked out my acres and planted some shade trees, and I watered them by carrying water up the hill on my back."

When Togni came to the benchland, he found "some Folle Blanche, Thompson Seedless and Aligoté. And down the driveway from the house and left of it, there were two ancient vines of Rose of Peru, also called Black Prince. These were head pruned, and they were the most exquisite eating grapes. There were also some fig trees and some olive trees."

But most of all, Togni found Will Silvear's then decades-old Pinot Noir,

Pinot Blanc, Chardonnay and Chenin Blanc vineyards. That year, 1960, under numbingly difficult conditions, Philip Togni used these four varieties to make the first wine ever produced on the benchland property.

With the first wine, the name Chalone came into being. Philip Togni knew nothing about the Chalone Indian tribe that once lived in the mountain range, but he believed a winery's name should be specific. "The more local the name, the more you explain," he said. "But right there above the benchland was this rather humpy peak called Mount Chalone. I told Liska and Sigman, that's what we should call the winery—Mount Chalone."

The name along with a license application was sent to the Bureau of Alcohol, Tobacco and Firearms in Washington. It was rejected. There was already a Mount Chalone, the letter said, but it went on to suggest they name the winery Chalone, Inc.

On July 11, 1961, Chalone, Inc. became a corporation authorized to issue 100,000 shares of common stock at the par value of $1 per share. The corporation had three directors; Edward Liska, John Sigman and John E. Sullivan, Sigman's lawyer.

"Inc. looks terrible on a label," Togni commented. "So while Chalone, Inc. became the official name, unofficially we called it Chalone Vineyard."

The partners now had a name for the winery. With the arrival of Togni, they also had wine. But the conditions under which the wine was made were problematic to say the least. These problems began in the vineyard. "Armbrister's idea of pruning was to cut every shoot back to two buds. By the time I started, the vines were covered with little spurs," Togni said. Another problem was that there had been no significant planting since Will Silvear put in the original vines, although it seemed that Armbrister had tried. "I found little bundles of cuttings all over the place," Togni added. "He would just stick them in the ground; I suppose he thought they would root. Of course they wouldn't do any such thing."

There was also the problem of the grape-loving deer, demanding that one of Togni's first tasks was to build a fence. And if all of that wasn't enough, with less than 10 inches of rain that year, there was a serious lack of water.

"There was a well that gave at best 2,000 gallons a day," Togni said. "The school at Davis said if you could put just five gallons of water on a vine in the rainy season, it would help. So I put empty wine barrels on the tractor and filled them with water; then I towed them around the vineyards. But the incline was too steep; the barrels rolled off the tractor and down the hill. It was a disaster."

"There was a hardware store in Soledad." Togni said. "The man who owned it also owned a lot of land around Chalone, and he had dug wells on every one of his properties. But he had no success; not one of them gave him water. It was said that he spent more money digging for water than he paid for the land." The people at Chalone had no money to dig a well, so they bought an old redwood water tank in Morgan Hill, hauled it up to the benchland on a truck and set it in a notch on the hill.

Out of 35 acres of vineyards, Togni said, he harvested only 16 tons of grapes in 1960—about half a ton per acre. Most of the Chenin Blanc—the last of the four varieties to ripen—was sold. The rest of the Chenin Blanc and all the Chardonnay, Pinot Noir and Pinot Blanc were destined to be made into Chalone's first wines. But where? Another problem: Liska and Sigman didn't have the money to build a winery.

Togni looked around at what was there, and he improvised. The chicken coop where Will Silvear once developed his new breed of capon was a low space about 11 feet wide and 40 feet long. That, Togni decided, would be the Chalone winery, "probably the narrowest winery in the state of California." He cleaned it out; then he cleared a flat space along the outer wall, poured concrete into it and put a gutter along one side and a little step up.

He bought a hand crusher to which he geared a gasoline engine and installed it on the new concrete slab. From the crusher, the grapes went into a basket press. All the wines—red and white—were fermented and aged in old Port barrels that Togni had bought from the Paul Masson winery for $15 each. "Not the greatest thing in which to make Chardonnay," he said. "I did lots of hard scrubbing of those barrels."

The next challenge was how to rack the wine. There was no electricity at Chalone, but Togni, who had worked for a while in Bordeaux, remembered seeing how wine was pumped from barrel to barrel in the *chais* of the Médoc. "So I thought we could do that here with a pressure cylinder. I devised a way in which I could push gas from a cylinder with a regulator into a barrel and displace the wine. I didn't know then that it was actually a terribly superior way of doing it because with displaced gas, there's no oxidation."

In 1961 when the first wines were ready, Ed Liska, his wife, Claire, and their five-year-old daughter bottled them under Togni's supervision.

The 1960 harvest produced 600 cases of wine. The bottles bore Chalone's first label, designed by Arthur Baker, a calligrapher in Berkeley, California, and printed by chef, restaurateur and "renaissance man" Narsai David on a parchment-like paper. In black and white, it depicted a silhouette of Mount Chalone in the background, and while alterations in the lettering and a few refinements have been made over the years, the label so clearly represents Chalone that the basic design remains virtually the same today.

Meanwhile, Liska continued as a weekend carpenter. Soon, others joined him. David Early, who had met Jack Sigman in San Francisco a few years before, recalled how "a group of us would go to Chalone on weekends and help. They became nail and hammer weekends for a lot of professional people; we seemed to need it, banging our thumbs and cutting ourselves. It was a way of getting away from our everyday work."

While weekends may have been filled with camaraderie and cheer, the weeks were filled with simplicity and quiet but also hard labor under devastating conditions, Philip Togni remembered: "There were two buildings—a house and a barn. I had a room in the house. Jack Armbrister was still with us. In winter he would tie chains onto the tires of his car with strings to hold it on the muddy road when he drove down to Soledad." By then the road that was to become Highway 146 to the Pinnacles had been built along Shirttail Canyon; but it was not yet paved.

Other than Armbrister, Togni had a couple of other neighbors on the benchland. There was a woman named Nettie Mathiesen, whose property bordered Chalone. And there was a man called Robie Espinosa, who some days said his mother had been Indian and his father Spanish and other days claimed he was the last full-blooded Chalone Indian. He lived in a little wooden hut on the other side of Chalone. "We were only 11 miles up the range," Togni said, "but it felt at least a thousand miles from anywhere."

Peggy Tamm also lived on the benchland, on the land she had inherited from her husband Charles in 1950; it lay at the end of Stonewall Canyon Road to the west of Chalone, the olive grove Charles had planted still visible.

PHILIP TOGNI HAD NOT STARTED OUT TO BE A WINEMAKER. Born in England, the son of an English mother and father from Switzerland's Ticino region, he studied geology and saw his future as prospecting for oil in places like Borneo or Colombia or Venezuela. But he also noticed that most oil geologists retired at age 55 and died about three years later. "Dying at 58 did not appeal to me, so I began to think about what else there was in life," Togni said.

On a trip to Jerez in the south of Spain, Togni met Señor Gonzalez of the Sherry-producing family. After talking over his future with him, Señor Gonzalez suggested Togni talk to Professor Maynard Amerine, who was with the University of California at Davis and happened to be in Madrid at the moment. "So I trotted up there and, sure enough, I met Amerine on the Plaza del Sol. We sat down to chat and he says, yes, you can study grape growing and winemaking. There are four places to do it: Davis in California, Geisenheim in Germany, or Montpelier and Bordeaux in France. He told me to look up a friend of his in Bordeaux. So I took a train to Bordeaux and, when I got off, a man comes forward and says, 'Mr. Lichine is away but please come out and see what we have.'

I sat there at Château Prieuré-Lichine and drank wine and ate and looked over the vineyards. I was impressed.

"I went back to England, counted my money and knew I'd never get to Davis. I didn't speak German so Geisenheim was out. The fees at Montpelier were modest, so I wrote and told them I was coming," Togni said.

Togni studied at Montpelier in southwest France for three years but left before receiving his diploma. He worked in a giant cooperative near Montpelier. "I thought winemaking was going to be little groups stomping grapes," he said. "Here was a hellhole of tall concrete tanks piled on top of each other and catwalks; it was like a scene from the underworld."

Togni visited wineries in Italy, Burgundy and Alsace. He went to Algeria, where he blended wine for six months. And then came a letter from Alexis Lichine asking, "Why don't you come and help us here?"

In Bordeaux Togni worked at Prieuré-Lichine and studied under Emile Peynaud at the University of Bordeaux. After he got his diploma in enology in 1957, he made wine in Chile for a year and then thought, "What next?"

Next, as it turned out, was California. He became production manager at Mayacamas Vineyards, high in the mountains above Napa, for a year. During that time, he met Walter Richert, who had a winery in Santa Clara County. It was Richert who told him about the property on the benchland above Soledad.

Togni was clearly an experienced winemaker by the time he met Liska and Sigman. He was young, idealistic, educated, energetic and enthusiastic. He was also in need of money.

Chalone, in fact, had no money at all. "My agreement with Liska and Sigman was that to start, I would receive $250 a month. After six months, I would get $300 a month," Togni said. "And there were the five acres. Nothing grabs me more than the idea of owning a piece of land—even if this piece had no trees except what I had just planted and even if it was stuck out in nowhere. They must have known how important it was to me. But right from the beginning, even my monthly salary was rarely paid. I worked on a shoestring. Once, when I was down to 10 cents, I drove up to San Francisco and hammered on Sigman's door shouting, 'When are you going to pay me?' "

The 1961 harvest did nothing to help Togni's situation. The winter rainfall, always sparse, was even lower then Chalone's normal, and the weed growth in the vineyards sucked up what little moisture there was. The vines struggled through the season; in the end, the production from 35 acres was a total of only 1.5 tons of grapes. "It was a non-harvest. I tried to buy grapes but in 1961, there were none to buy. Finally, we bought some bulk wine from Mirassou and aged and finished it at Chalone," Togni said.

By 1962, with his salary always late, Togni began to look for a way out. "I'd ask Sigman for the money he owed me. He was an easygoing, accommodating kind of a guy, one of those people who said yes to everything; the only trouble was, he didn't always come through. Yes, he'd say, we'll send you a check. Or yes, Ed and I are taking these 600 cases up to our basements in San Francisco, and we'll be selling them. Then we'll pay you. But he didn't. He wasn't as solid as Liska."

After a while, too, the isolation of the benchland began to overwhelm Togni. There was no one there involved in winemaking, no one in viticulture, and no one to whom he could relate. Soledad offered little more. It was populated by employees of the nearby state prison and by non-English-speaking laborers on the valley's ranches. And in the grocery store, Togni found, he was on the book not by name but as "the pruner in the hills." By then, too, he had met Birgitta Pehrsson and wanted to marry her.

He found his way out of Chalone when he met Dimitri Tchelistcheff, son of André Tchelistcheff, who was doing varietal studies at Gallo. Dimitri was leaving, he told Togni, and Gallo needed someone to replace him. On August 1, 1962, Togni went to work for Gallo in Modesto, but he did not desert Chalone. Working there on weekends and with the help of Rodney Strong, he brought in the 1962 harvest and made his last wine on the benchland.

By 1962 Edward Liska also wanted to be free of Chalone. "Our idea was great, but Sigman and I were naïve," Liska said. "We had no idea how much money it would take to run Chalone and how long it would be before it produced income. It required more sophisticated structuring than we had."

He offered to sell his half of Chalone to Sigman, and Sigman agreed to buy it. On November 1, 1962, Jack Sigman signed a promissory note stipulating that he would pay Edward and Claire Liska $9,900.

"Sigman was a good salesman with a direct manner, good eye contact and a good handshake," Liska said. "He had such a persuasive manner that you really believed him when he said he mailed the check yesterday or would mail it tomorrow."

But Sigman never did mail a check to Liska. For the next three years, Liska tried to collect his money. When nothing else worked, Liska's lawyers put a lien on a house Sigman owned on Palm Street in San Francisco. Sigman's lawyer immediately called Liska's lawyer, begging them to withdraw the lien. If they didn't, he said, Sigman threatened to kill himself. Liska withdrew the lien. Sigman did not kill himself. Nor did he pay Liska. At the same time that Liska was trying to collect his money from Sigman, Togni was trying to collect his money from both of them.

Chalone still owed Togni $1,200. "I went to see Robert Brown, a lawyer in Modesto who talked about 'piercing the corporate veil' to reach the money. But the corporation had no money." Togni sued Sigman and Liska, and the case was heard at the Municipal Court in Salinas. Liska was there; Sigman did not respond to the suit. On June 22, 1965, the judge ruled that Liska and Sigman were personally responsible only until the date of incorporation. Therefore, they, as the partnership doing business as El Venido, must pay Togni $500 plus seven percent interest from July 7, 1961, plus costs of $60.80. Liska paid Togni his share. Sigman paid nothing.

With the Togni suit settled, Liska's attorneys and accountant advised him, he said, "to stop wasting my time and money. And that's how it ended. I paid Togni. I paid my attorneys. I lost my share of Chalone and the $9,900 plus five percent interest. I've been a psychiatrist for over 40 years. Sigman became a clinical curiosity to me, a curious paradox. The last time I saw him was in 1963. After 1965, I never saw Chalone again either."

4 | *Rodney Strong and Long-Distance Winemaking*

RODNEY STRONG, A FORMER DANCER AND CHOREOGRAPHER, managed a small wine shop called Tiburon Vintners in Tiburon, across the Golden Gate Bridge from San Francisco. He also managed a then small winery, Windsor Vineyards, in northern Sonoma County. One of his customers at the wine shop was Jack Sigman, who had a house on nearby Corinthian Island. Because Sigman owned Chalone, the two spent a good deal of time in the shop talking about wine. One day Sigman asked Strong if he might be interested in doing something with his little vineyards above Soledad.

"So, reluctantly, one day I drove the 220 miles to Soledad," Strong said, "driving up an incredibly narrow gravel road to this godforsaken place near the Pinnacles National Monument. It was spectacular. When I got there, I met this very charming fellow, Philip Togni. Philip had amassed bare bones there. He had no budget, no money. There was no electricity. He had to start up a generator to do anything at all. There was almost no water. The vines were suffering dramatically. The deer and the rabbits were getting most of the grapes. The problems were endemic. And I absolutely loved it. I thought it was great. And I was fascinated by the hillside vineyards. It was in some ways what everyone expects a vineyard to look like." Togni offered Strong a tasting of his Chalone wines—

35

Chardonnay, Pinot Noir, Pinot Blanc and Chenin Blanc. Strong liked what he tasted.

Soon after, Sigman asked Strong to come to Chalone for the 1962 harvest to help make wine. By the fall, he explained, Togni would be working at Gallo and could only be at Chalone part time during the vintage. Since the grapes at Chalone came in earlier than those in the more northern Windsor Vineyards, Strong agreed to do it.

"I went down there pretty much as Philip's assistant," Strong said. "We picked the grapes in boxes, brought them back to the little chicken coop and pressed them in an old hand press. Then we put the juice in barrels and put gunnysacks filled with ice on top of the barrels to cool them down during fermentation. It was primitive winemaking."

It was primitive living, too. One morning, Strong woke up to find 18 baby rattlesnakes in the front room. "A mother rattlesnake had given birth during the night. But there were other lovely things. And whenever I looked up there was always this incredible jagged range of the Pinnacles. So I worked with Philip, and he was very kind to me. I learned a lot from him. At the end of the harvest, he went back to Gallo; he had too much talent not to do things properly. And I went back to Windsor," Strong said.

Rodney Strong left his home state of Washington in 1945 to study dance with Balanchine in New York. He went on to dance with the New York City Ballet and to choreograph for the Latin Quarter nightclub. From there, he went to Paris, where he choreographed for the Bluebell dancers. By the mid-1950s, knowing a dancer's professional life is short, he and his wife, Charlotte, moved to California intent on starting a new career in wine. He began by working briefly for Richert & Sons Winery, where he did basic cellar work—from dragging hoses to racking barrels. Coincidentally, Richert was the man who first told Philip Togni about the benchland property on Gavilan. He was also the vintner who first saw a loophole in the law that allowed anyone with a winegrower's license to open a wine shop away from the winery premises. He opened a shop in Carmel then another in Tiburon, hiring his former cellar worker, Rodney Strong, to run it.

"I was so poor at the time that, for money, I not only ran Tiburon Vintners, I also taught dancing and did choreography and some gigs in San Francisco," Strong said. "One of the places that hired me was a private club called The Family. I put on shows there using their members, and, for these shows, I would teach some of the business types to do sexy little numbers like the side-cross step. One of the members in my show was Russ Graff. That was 1959."

A short time before Strong met him, Russell Graff, Bill Moore and Suren Saroyan had joined Byron Nishkian in buying a 160-acre property in Windsor, in northern Sonoma County. The property had belonged to the Williams family, cousins of Elvira Nishkian, Byron's wife, and had a farmhouse on it as well as vineyards and a winery. "But we weren't particularly interested in making wine; we bought the property for the land," Russ Graff said. "It was the first of several joint real estate ventures the four of us made. In all our ventures, we acquired properties not for what was on them, but principally for the value of the land."

After directing Graff in one of the shows at The Family, Strong struck up a friendship with him. When he learned that Graff was involved in the Windsor property and that one of the Williamses had stayed on as winemaker but the wine was poor, Strong proposed that he run the property. Graff and his partners agreed, and Rod and Charlotte moved to Windsor.

Strong had limited experience in winemaking. Other than working briefly for Richert & Sons, he had completed a short apprenticeship in Europe and had taken some enology courses at the University of California at Davis. But because he had worked in Chalone's 1962 harvest with Philip Togni and because George Marriott, whose 1963 wines were never bottled under the Chalone label, had left, Sigman asked Strong to take over winemaking at Chalone. "And typical of me—I go where angels fear to tread—I said yes. Actually, I had grown to love the area. It was the most exciting, the sexiest area in the world. There aren't many places like that anymore," Strong said.

The agreement Sigman made with the owners of Windsor Vineyards was that Windsor would make wine from Chalone's grapes. In a lease that was very favorable to Windsor, the Sonoma winery would buy Chalone's entire inventory—both the bottled wines currently in stock and wine in bulk—for 50 cents a gallon.

Strong hadn't forgotten the experience of making wine with Togni in 1962. "Conditions at Chalone were so rustic that, as much as I loved the place, I said that from now on, we'll pick the grapes and haul them up to Windsor to vinify." The wines made from Chalone's grapes were bottled under the Windsor label or as private-label wines, a major part of Windsor's business.

During the year, Rod Strong would finish work at Windsor on Friday at 5 p.m., drive his truck down to Chalone, arrive close to midnight and spend the weekend working in the vineyards. "We made very nice Pinot Noir, Chardonnay and Chenin Blanc from Chalone's grapes. We also made Folle Blanche, which we sold in the Windsor tasting room. But I was getting beaten to a frazzle going down there on weekends. And there just weren't enough grapes to make it worthwhile," Strong said.

Nor was there enough water. "We had some water engineers drill holes, but everything was dry. We were losing our buns on Chalone, and I could see no way of our ever making money down there," Strong said. "Sigman didn't know much about wine. As long as somebody would take care of Chalone for him, he was all right. But he didn't want any trouble. Meanwhile, Windsor was going gangbusters. Those were wonderful times. They were the adventurous, swashbuckling wine years in California."

GEORGE MARRIOTT KNEW NOTHING ABOUT WINE except that he enjoyed it. After earning a degree in English literature in 1960, he returned to his hometown of Chicago and drove a taxi, much to his father's consternation. So he moved to San Francisco and drove a taxi there. One day late in 1961, a friend, Joshua Freiwald, told him how he had helped at Chalone one weekend. Marriott found Freiwald's description of Chalone so enchanting that he got into his 1941 Oldsmobile ("It cost me $100.") and drove to the benchland.

No one was there. He walked around the winery and through the vineyards, touching the dormant vines and wondering aloud, "That's what a grapevine looks like?" He left a note on the old iron gate saying he'd like to work for free on his days off. Sigman found the note, zeroed in on the word "free" and wrote a note to Togni: "I'd like you to meet this chap who wants to work for nothing."

Togni and Marriott met in San Francisco and soon Marriott was helping Togni around the vineyards and winery—for free. "Philip taught me a lot. He was very exacting, very demanding. He was a marvelous tutor," Marriott said.

After Togni left Chalone, Sigman offered Marriott a full-time job. "Cab driving was safe in those days, and by working long hours, I was making $250, $300 a week," Marriott said. "After a lot of negotiating with Sigman, he offered me $150 a month plus a room. As it turned out, even that $150 wasn't always paid."

In 1963, with neither Togni nor Strong there to make wine, Marriott became the winemaker—by the book. "Philip had given me a text by Amerine. I read it by Coleman lamp. You need yeast for fermenting? I drove to town and got Fleischmann's Yeast. You need analysis? I brought samples down to the lab at the San Martin Winery. We had no lab and even if we had had one, I wouldn't have known how to use it," Marriott said.

"When the Chenin Blanc fermentation stuck, I'd siphon the wine out into the sun to warm up so it would start fermenting again; then I'd siphon it back into the barrel. If it got too hot, I'd get into this really old truck and drive to the valley for ice. The doors of the truck would fly open so I had to hold the door on the driver's side shut while I was driving. I'd get the ice back to the winery and put it on top of the

39

barrel to cool the wine down, and it would start fermenting again. Anyway, it took three months for the Chenin Blanc to finish fermenting. I worked hard. I'm not very organized, but I really put myself to the test on that one."

One day in the midst of Marriott's intensive solo harvest the Soledad fire department came rushing up with bells clanging. "We heard there was a fire up here," the firemen told Marriott. No, there wasn't; but what they were really saying, Marriott suspected, was that they'd like some wine. A couple of days later, they came rushing up again. "Heard you had a fire, they said." This time, Marriott was prepared. He gave them a gallon—half bulk wine, half vinegar. "They never came back, but I don't know what the bottle did for Chalone's reputation," Marriott said.

Marriott would sometimes take a bottle of bulk wine and join Jack Armbrister, Robie Espinosa and Nettie Mathiesen, who was a teetotaler, for a game of cards. "We'd sit down by kerosene lamp and play cards and holler at each other. We were in the middle of nowhere, nothing was going on, there were no other sounds, but we'd holler at each other. They were my only company," Marriott said.

"I was living up there alone with no electricity, no phone. About once a week, I'd go to Soledad for supplies. But Sigman never paid our accounts so I'd be approached by people all over town saying if we didn't pay, they'd sue. There was never enough money, even for basics. There was a beautiful old barn, but it was in bad condition. I kept asking for money to buy some 2x4s so I could tie it together. But I didn't get the money, and one day, it blew down, on top of the tractor. I began to think about looking for another job," he said.

A year and a half after he went to work full time at Chalone, George Marriott left, but like Togni before him and others who would follow, he left with indelible memories.

"When someone is totally in a place, he goes through a period believing he's on a spot on the earth where there is no way to communicate with the outside world," Marriott said. "Chalone had that quality. Everything about it had the silhouette of aloneness. It suited me at that time. It was a wonderful wedding of my feelings and that place. So my endearment for Chalone is much, much more than just my experience with winemaking. It is the wine that gets the attention, but what I remember most was simply the quality of being in a place like that."

PART TWO

❧

Evolution Leads
to a New Beginning

5 | *Richard Graff Comes to Chalone*

RICHARD (DICK) GRAFF WAS THE OLDEST of Russ Graff's four sons. Richard and David, two years apart, were born in Connecticut. After the family moved to California early in World War II, John and then Peter Graff were born.

Like his father, Dick Graff attended Harvard. Unlike his father, who had studied civil structural engineering, Dick's field of concentration at Harvard was music. After graduation, he joined the U.S. Navy; in the next three years, he went to officer candidate school and became, first, an antisubmarine officer and, next, a gunnery officer on a destroyer. At the same time, he continued his interest in music, moving a portable organ aboard ship and training a chorus made up of members of the crew. Later, when the ship was docked in the Philippines, he took the chorus to perform in churches.

While music was his love, Dick never planned to make it his profession. And when he left the Navy in 1963, he had to consider what, in fact, he would do for a career. Looking back on his family's professional history gave him no immediate clues; like his father, his paternal grandfather had been an engineer, while his maternal grandfather had been an artist. After considering various fields, Dick decided on bank management and became a management trainee at Union Bank in Los Angeles.

While he was in the Navy, Dick's parents had divorced and his father had remarried. One weekend in 1964, Dick went north to visit his father. While he was there, Russ Graff took him to the Windsor Vineyards winery. "I had never been to a winery before," Dick said. "And except for a wine course I had taken with Nathan Chroman in Los Angeles, I knew nothing about wine. Rod Strong showed me around, and I was fascinated."

After the tour, Charlotte Strong served lunch on the terrace surrounded by vineyards, and Rod poured some early-1960s Chalone Chardonnay, Pinot Blanc and Chenin Blanc. Dick tasted the wines and listened to stories about Chalone. By the time Rod mentioned that Sigman might want to sell the property, Dick was entranced—and interested.

He returned to Los Angeles and called his friend, Peter Panaaker, who had inherited money from his mother and had built a four-condominium building at Laguna Beach. "I didn't have the money," Dick said, "but I was intrigued with the idea of buying Chalone, even before I saw it." He went town to Laguna Beach to talk with Panaaker about Chalone. Peter was also intrigued, and mused about wanting to have a vineyard. They arranged to meet Rod Strong at Chalone one weekend in the summer of 1964.

The two drove up in Dick's 1951 Chevrolet. "Peter thought it would not be a good idea to appear in his Bentley; it might convey the wrong impression," Dick said. As they wound their way up the dirt road from Soledad, they met Rod, who was out shooting rabbits.

"Rod showed us around, and I fell in love with the place," Dick remembered. "We went back to the little house that Ed Liska had built. It was pretty bare, with not much more than a built-in bench all around the main room. I supposed it was for sleeping. And in each corner, there was an ungainly cabinet. The house had been wired for electricity, but there wasn't even a generator there at that time. We moved the table out on the porch. Rod fixed dinner and we ate on the deck with a kerosene lamp for light."

By the time he and Panaaker left the benchland, Dick Graff could envision a future other than bank management.

Dick was, in fact, determined to get Chalone and at first assumed it would be rather easy. "Rod said Sigman was now eager to sell," Dick said. "After seeing the place, Peter was excited about buying it. So we put together a plan. Peter would supply the money. Rod would provide the viticulture and winemaking expertise. And I would do the work."

It all sounded great, but when they presented their plan to Russ Graff and his partners, they ran into a brick wall. The plan could work only if Windsor was willing to give up its lease with Chalone. Rod, who would have been delighted to have the Sonoma winery drop the lease, was an employee of Windsor and had no say in the decision. Russ Graff was in favor of the idea, and so was Bill Moore. However, Byron Nishkian and Suren Saroyan were not. The two men would be willing to cancel the lease, they said, only if they were given residual interest in Chalone and a share of the profits. Negotiations dragged on until Peter Panaaker lost interest.

In the meantime, Jack Sigman had bought the Paso Robles Inn, about 75 miles south of Chalone. Because Dick wanted so much to be part of Chalone and because he did not know how else he could do it, he drove to Paso Robles and introduced himself to Jack Sigman, saying, "I suspect you really don't want to sell Chalone." Sigman admitted that he was selling it reluctantly. "I asked him not to sell it, to take me on as a partner," Dick said. "I told him I would go to Davis to study wine-making and viticulture, and I would pay him as soon as the winery began to make money."

Sigman listened. Days passed, and finally he agreed. "What about Chalone's agreement with Windsor?" Dick asked. Don't worry, Sigman assured him—he would shed the lease. A friend of his would then buy the property back, and Sigman would buy it back from him. He would have to give his unnamed friend 5 percent of the place, he added, and then he and Dick would split the difference.

Previously, Sigman had mortgaged the property for $13,000. In June

1965, he defaulted on payments he owed on the mortgage, which forced the property into foreclosure and nullified the lease that Windsor held. Sigman's friend then purchased the foreclosed property. Next, Sigman borrowed $13,000 from the Bank of America in Paso Robles to pay the $13,000 purchase price, and the title of Chalone was transferred to his friend.

The following month, a partnership was formed, in which Dick and David Early, as Sigman's nominee, each received 47.5 percent. "At that time, Sigman was up against the wall," Early said. "He had Chalone in his left pocket and didn't want the IRS to know about it. No one was paying withholding taxes for the employees at the Paso Robles Inn. So he transferred his entire paper worth of Chalone to my name to hold for him for a while."

In the same month, Dick and Sigman drew up an interest-bearing promissory note, in which Dick agreed to pay $22,325 to Sigman for his 47.5 percent of Chalone out of the monies that would eventually come to him as the winery became profitable. It was understood, although not stated in the note, that it was to be a long-term arrangement. Sigman also agreed verbally not to assign the note and to renew it annually.

In September 1965 the partners incorporated. Dick received 7,790 shares (47.5 percent), David Early received an equal number of shares as Sigman's nominee and Sigman's friend received 820 shares (5 percent). The new corporation was named Chalone Vineyard, Ltd.

SIGMAN'S FRIEND AND NEW 5-PERCENT OWNER OF CHALONE was Danforth Field II. Field had met Sigman in the late 1950s while he was in the mutual funds business and Sigman was still a stockbroker with Reynolds & Co. "John would talk about wine, and, although I didn't know much about it, I enjoyed drinking wine," Field said. "I still have one of Chalone's original bottles, the Chenin Blanc 1960."

"In 1960, John asked me to put some money into the winery. I gave him $1,000 here, $1,000 there over the next two or three years," Field said. "Altogether, I put $5,000 into the corporation. I was also selling wine for Chalone. I'd go to Ed Liska's house in San Francisco and pick up cases and then sell them, mostly to stockbrokers. I bought some myself and used them as a sales promotion; when one of my guys did a good job, I would give him a bottle of Chalone. In those days we sold the Chardonnay for about $3.50 a bottle, Pinot Blanc for $3 and Chenin Blanc for $2. I never had any Pinot Noir. Anyway, after I sold the wine, I would turn the money over to Sigman. I didn't get anything out of it."

Field's involvement with Chalone deepened, he said, after a visit he and his wife, Jennie, made one day when they were in Napa Valley. "One of the stockbrokers I knew well told me about Souverain Cellars and Lee Stewart. So when we were up there, I stopped by Souverain and knocked on the door," Field said. "Lee was an interesting man, very aloof; and when he came to the door, he said, 'We don't have a tasting room here.' But when I mentioned how much I liked his wines and that I was also involved in a small way with Chalone, he became very friendly. He said Chalone wine was superb. I gave him a bottle of Chalone Chardonnay and he gave me a bottle of Souverain Cabernet Sauvignon." It was Stewart's admiration of Chalone, according to Field, that encouraged him to become still further involved with Sigman.

"I look back and realize I never received any shares in hand, and I never asked John for any," Field said. "I just gave him money and said I wanted to be part of the winery. And he said, 'You have a total of 5 percent of the corporation.' That all happened before Dick Graff came into the picture."

Shortly before Dick met Sigman, Dick's maternal grandfather had died, leaving an inheritance to his three daughters. When Dick became Sigman's partner, he borrowed $25,000 from his mother, Estelle, for Chalone. The money was secured as a deed of trust at Security First National Bank, acting as trustee to Estelle Graff. Of the $25,000, Sigman received $18,000, of which $13,000 was intended to repay the money he had borrowed from the Bank of America in Paso Robles. It was later revealed that Sigman never repaid the loan. The remaining $7,000 of the $25,000 was to be used as working capital for Chalone. As a lien on the property, the deed was the senior obligation—that is, in a case of multiple debts it would be paid before anything else. Because Estelle Graff knew Chalone had no money, she waived amortization of the principal for three years, asking only that interest payments be made.

Soon after Sigman agreed to take on Dick as a partner, Dick left his $450-per-month management training job in Los Angeles and moved to Paso Robles. "Sigman had bought the inn with a woman friend, Maricella Koons. But he leased out the most profitable part—the restaurant and bar," Dick said. "He was going broke on the inn part, and he didn't have much help. So he had me there to help out. I did mostly maintenance and gardening." During the time he owned the inn, Jack Sigman rented a house on Oak Street in Paso Robles. Sigman's father, visiting him from Chicago, stayed there with him and worked at the inn with Dick.

David Early also worked at the Paso Robles Inn as a night desk clerk. Before Early became Sigman's nominee in the corporation, he was an investor in Chalone. "After Dr. Liska sold his shares, Jack was trying to get investors," Early said. "I put in about $4,000 or $5,000. It was supposed to get me one acre of the property. A number of people invested. Our money, we were told, was to be used as working capital for the winery. I never actually had any of my shares in hand. I believed that they were kept by the corporation."

In the fall of 1964, before Dick became a partner, he had taken part in his first Chalone harvest, as a picker. "It was a complete disaster," he said. "Most of the grapes had been eaten by the birds. Rod had us go through and pick what we could in case there were a few grapes that hadn't been pecked open. Whatever we did harvest was taken north to Sonoma County." At that time, Chalone's harvests were still under contract with Windsor.

In the fall of 1965, free of its lease with Windsor, Chalone sold its grape harvest to Mirassou. That fall, too, Dick left the Paso Robles Inn for the University of California at Davis to begin his studies in viticulture and enology. For a while, David Early assumed Dick's job as gardener at the inn until he left to take a job as a dental technician in San Francisco.

⁊

DICK'S STUDENT DAYS AT DAVIS WERE DAYS OF HAPPY TRANQUILITY. He was studying to be a winemaker. He was studying French. And with a nod to his musical background, he was taking a course in orchestral conducting. It was also during this time that he met Darrell Corti. Darrell's family owned a large food and wine retail business in nearby Sacramento, and Darrell managed the wine division, Corti Brothers Fine Wines. A brilliant student of wine, Darrell was interested in Dick's involvement in Chalone, and he often invited him to have dinner with his family. "Darrell's mother would cook wonderful Italian meals, and Darrell would pull great, great wines out of his cellar," Dick recalled.

One evening at the Corti home, Dick met Bob Nikkel. The owner of a successful lumber business, Nikkel had had a long romance with wine. "From the time I was nine years old until I was 20, I worked in vineyards in the San Joaquin Valley in central California," he said. "During that time—especially in my teens—I thought, someday I'd like to benefit from the final product of all this work." It took a while, but by the late 1950s, after he was established in lumbering, Bob Nikkel began to pursue wine as the hobby. Like Darrell, he was intrigued by Dick's stories about Chalone. When Dick invited him to visit the winery some weekend, Nikkel nodded that he just might do that.

But not everything in Dick's life was perfect. By mid-semester, Dick was beset with financial problems. "I was running out of money," he said. "I asked Sigman for help, but he said, 'I don't have any money.' I didn't know what else to do so I applied for a student loan and, luckily, I was able to get one, enough to carry me through the balance of the year."

That spring Darrell bought Chalone's 1960 Chardonnay, Pinot Blanc and Chenin Blanc, held a public tasting of the wines and offered them for sale in his family's wine shop. The day after the tasting, Corti drove to Chalone for the first time.

At the end of the academic year, Dick took a job as a pile driver with a company his father owned in Northern California. The work was hard but the pay was good, and he was able to return to Chalone on weekends, where he lived in the house that Ed Liska built. And so it was a summer of weekdays driving piles with all the attendant noise and heat and power, and weekends on the benchland in primitive silence.

Bob Nikkel did not forget Dick's invitation to visit Chalone. One weekend during the summer of 1966, he and his brother drove down for a visit. "It was apparent to me," Nikkel said, "that Dick was really struggling. I wanted to find a way to help him." In the years that would follow, Bob Nikkel would find many such opportunities.

Midway through August of 1966, the grapes were getting ripe, and there was a great deal of work to do to get the winery ready for the first full harvest. So, Dick left his pile-driving job to work at the winery full time. By the time Dick had finished at UC-Davis, all of the Corti family had become interested in his Chalone venture, and as the 1966 harvest neared, they all offered to help. Frank Corti, Darrell's father, spent his two-week vacation working at Chalone. Darrell's sister and brother, Illa and Daniel, came to Chalone to work, and so, of course, did Darrell. And Darrell's mother came to Chalone one day to see what her family was doing.

So, Dick had his winery and harvest work crew, but no money. How would he finance the harvest? "By selling a barrel of 1966 Chardonnay—not yet made—to my sister, Illa, as a future," Darrell recounted. "I talked her into buying one barrel—that's 60 gallons—at $10 a gallon. Her $600 was the seed money for Chalone's 1966 harvest."

Next, the crew needed to prepare the little chicken coop winery. Dick, Darrell and the other workers insulated it, put in a ceiling where there had previously been only the roof, and painted the entire interior with epoxy paint. They took apart the press, sandblasted it and repainted it with epoxy paint. They washed down every other piece of equipment and epoxied all the screws and other metal fittings and fixtures in the winery.

At the end of this two-week "vacation," Frank Corti returned to work at Corti Brothers. But Darrell, Illa, Daniel and Dick's mother, Estelle Graff, stayed on. With all they had done, there was still much more to do. They had to find picking boxes. They had to buy clippers. They had to line up a picking crew. And they had to prepare the barrels.

While Dick was at Davis, he purchased 50 French oak barrels from Siruge, a fine Burgundian cooper, in anticipation of the 1966 harvest. Now the barrels were at Chalone, and in need of work. First, the staves had to be tightened. That was done by putting burlap sacks over the heads of the barrels, wetting them and letting the water run down, to swell the wood. After about a week of this treatment, the barrels were ready to be soaked on the inside. As always, there was a shortage of water on the benchland, so Dick and Darrell loaded the barrels on the truck and took them down to the valley, where the Paul Masson winery gave them water and space. They filled the barrels and left them there for two weeks, while at Chalone they continued to prepare the winery. By the time the grapes were ripe enough to harvest, they had emptied the barrels, sulfured them to kill any bacteria and hauled them back to Chalone; now tightened, seasoned and cleaned, the barrels were hoisted onto the racks in the tiny winery.

"We finished cleaning and epoxying the day the harvest began," Darrell remembered, "actually, about an hour before the first boxes of white grapes arrived in the winery."

To pick grapes, Dick had lined up friends and family and a weekend crew from Paul Masson. He attached a sled to the tractor into which the pickers emptied their boxes of grapes. Chalone still had no electricity, but Dick had a generator, and he found an old Briggs & Stratton engine to run the crusher.

"But it was a crusher, not a stemmer," Darrell commented, "So we crushed the grapes with the stems and then pulled out the stems by hand."

When the engine was not working the crusher, it was pumping water out of the well. Dick also hooked the Briggs & Stratton engine to a small jet pump to move the fresh juice into the barrels. He put the white grape juice in barrels and the Pinot Noir juice in old, open puncheons. And fermentation began.

Just as the workers were finishing the harvest, they heard a roar and saw a cloud of dust on the Chalone road. And there, on a motorcycle, was Captain John Doench, The rank of "Captain," he claimed, was appropriate because he owned a diesel motor launch. But it wasn't during his time in the Navy that Dick Graff had met John Doench.

During the time that Dick was working at the Paso Robles Inn, Jack Sigman had bought a new blue convertible Corvette, which he put in Dick's name—"clearly, to keep it out of the hands of the creditors," Dick said. One day, while driving the Corvette down to Los Angeles for a weekend, Dick was stopped for speeding in Goleta, near Santa Barbara. "Admittedly, I was going fast along one clear, divided stretch of road—90 to 100 miles per hour." But the police claimed it was 120 miles per hour, and Dick was "detained" for a time in Goleta. While he was there, he met "Captain John," who had been arrested for writing bad checks. When Dick left Goleta, he said good-bye to Captain John and casually added that he should stop by Chalone some time. That was the last Dick had seen or heard of the Captain until he lumbered up the road to Chalone.

Immediately upon his arrival, Captain John made himself at home. Within days, he decided that what Dick needed most was a laboratory. In fact, Dick did need a lab, but there was no money for one. So Captain John persuaded Illa Corti to lend Chalone funds for a laboratory, and he would build it.

With the harvest completed, Dick went back to pile driving, this time in nearby Monterey. At about the same time, he became the agent for Siruge barrels in the United States. Until then, it was difficult for small wineries to purchase fine barrels. French oak wine barrels only began to come into California in the 1960s, and most of the companies that exported them insisted on larger minimum orders than were practical for the wineries at the time. Dick, on the other hand, allowed them to purchase as few barrels as they wished.

Meanwhile, Captain John was busy. Having ensconced himself at Chalone after the harvest, he built the laboratory. "He was certainly no master craftsman, but he did manage to get it up, and Illa paid the bills," Dick said.

With the laboratory complete, Captain John continued to live at Chalone. "While I was away working during the day, he would buzz around collecting building materials and, as it turned out, looking at property around Chalone." One evening when Dick returned, Captain John announced that he had just purchased a neighboring property that abutted Chalone. "He had made a deal with the woman who owned it but lived on the East Coast," Dick recalled. "He would buy the 160 acres for $10,000, nothing down, and pay her $1,000 a year. Immediately, he began buying things, all on credit. He bought a big diesel tractor with a plow. He bought a truck. He got a local fuel supplier to come up and install a diesel tank and a regular gas tank on the property. Everything on credit. He knew nothing about viticulture but he started plowing up some land to plant vineyards. Finally, when the creditors got too insistent, he just skipped. He has never been seen or heard from since."

But what was just one more adventure in the life of Captain John turned into a bit of serendipity for Dick Graff.

"Captain John had not paid as much as a penny for the property, so a year later, when I was able to negotiate with the owner, I bought the property myself." Dick said. "I paid her $2,000 plus seven percent interest to cover the two payments Captain John missed while he was living on the benchland. And I took up the contract for $10,000 with an agreement to pay it at $1,000 a year. This wasn't for the corporation. This was my own private property."

Dick would eventually develop vineyards on about eight acres of the property and build a house there.

6 | *Hard Times and a Long Fight*

FOR DICK GRAFF, planting a vineyard and building a home on his new property were still dreams far in the future. At the time of his purchase of the "Captain's" property, Dick was subsisting on very little money, and the initial payment of $2,000 plus interest was a large sum for him. It was about this time, in 1967, that Bob Nikkel again came to Dick's aid.

There was a 160-acre property that was separated from Chalone only by one other property. Originally owned by the Hall family and still called the Hall Ranch, it had been bought by Stanford Case. Now, Case wanted to sell it, and, while Dick could not afford to buy it, Bob Nikkel could. In another gesture of friendship, Nikkel purchased the property through his company, Lumber Investments, Ltd., for $19,000 and agreed to hold it until Dick could buy it from him at the price he paid plus 6 percent interest. Nikkel then hired Dick for $600 a month to take care of the Hall Ranch.

That same year, Nikkel also asked Dick to be a consultant to Mount Eden, a winery in Saratoga, about 150 miles northwest of Chalone. The pay was $250 a month. In the coming years, this arrangement was to be both boon and boondoggle for Bob Nikkel, Dick Graff and Chalone.

The man who founded Mount Eden, Martin Ray, entered Bob Nikkel's life in 1959. "He walked into my office, a roly-poly man, and by the time he left, I had bought seven cases of wine from him," Nikkel remembered. Two years later, when Nikkel and his wife visited him, Ray told them about his plan. Soon after Prohibition ended, Ray had bought the old Paul Masson winery in Saratoga and renamed it after himself. He later sold it to Seagram and, with the profit he made, bought 160 acres on a hillside, which he named Mount Eden; he planted part of it in Pinot Noir and Chardonnay. What he now planned to do was gather 25 people who would pay $10,000 each to become members of the Mount Eden Corporation. Nikkel signed up that day.

Over the years, as members would leave or Ray would throw them out of the group, he would ask Nikkel to buy their $10,000 shares. Soon Nikkel had controlling interest. Ray's purpose in starting Mount Eden Corporation was to have enough money to buy the adjacent 160 acres for himself, plant more vineyards and build a chateau for the members. He soon realized, however, that while 25 times $10,000 equaled $250,000, it was not going to be enough to keep his promises to the members.

Meanwhile, Ray was taking care of the vineyards and winemaking for the corporation. For his work, he was given half the production. He did eventually build a "chateau," which, according to Darrell Corti, was merely a building made of concrete set into the hillside. But he did not keep many of the other promises he made, and several members of the corporation became disenchanted.

"He ran the corporation like a fiefdom," Nikkel said. By the time Ray tried the ploy of putting his own property into the corporation in exchange for enough shares to give him majority control, most of the members said no.

A man known for his temper, Ray ordered everyone off the property, locked the gate and would neither care for the vineyards nor let their owners in to care for them.

"That's when Dick really saved me," said Nikkel, who by that time not only owned controlling interest in the corporation but also, at Ray's behest, had bought individual vineyards. Entering the property over the locked gate on the valley floor, Dick walked up the steep 2.5-mile dirt road and reconnoitered the property. He discovered he could get to the vineyards by going around, through Paul Masson property, and then cutting a path across, through the bush.

Dick, Bob Nikkel and a crew of Nikkel's lumber workers then drove up to Paul Masson, worked their way across to the Mount Eden vineyard and began pruning until Ray appeared with a sheriff. "Ray demanded the sheriff arrest us," Nikkel recalled. "Dick told the sheriff that Mr. Nikkel owned the vineyard and that if Mr. Ray disputed their right to be there, he should go through proper legal channels. The sheriff listened to Dick, then turned to Ray and suggested he leave. I've always been astounded by Dick's courage and moxie," Bob Nikkel said. That fall Nikkel and his crew picked the grapes and hauled them to Chalone where Dick made Mount Eden's wine.

The fight between the Mount Eden Corporation members and Martin Ray continued with Conger Fawcett, a young lawyer from San Francisco, leading the legal battle in the courts while Dick led the physical battle in the vineyards. The legal aspect was finally resolved in 1971 with the corporation retaining its original property on top of the hill, while Martin Ray was given the quarter section on which he had built his chateau. Dick Graff and Chalone would continue to be involved with Mount Eden for the next 11 years.

DICK'S PART IN THE MOUNT EDEN UPHEAVAL was only one of the many dramas that marked the years following the 1966 harvest. If the lack of money gnawed at Dick personally, it was even more acute for Chalone. The money that Estelle Graff had lent to Chalone had long been spent. Now, according to their agreement, Jack Sigman was supposed to provide working capital for the winery. To date he had not. Sigman was in serious financial trouble at the Paso Robles Inn and, he told Dick, had no money for Chalone. Nor had he taken over his shares in the Chalone corporation from David Early.

Since September 1965 when the corporation had been formed, Dick and Early had each sold 2.5 percent of Chalone's shares to Estelle Graff and 2.5 percent to Darrell Corti. This left Dick and David Early with 42.5 percent each, and Estelle and Darrell with 5 percent each.

Earlier that year, as the anniversary of their ownership agreement for Chalone approached, Sigman had Dick sign a renewal on Dick's promissory note to him. However, later that year Dick received a letter from Adrian Rose, a lawyer representing Otto Clegg, demanding Dick pay Clegg on his promissory note to Sigman. That was how Dick learned that the year before, on July 15, 1965, only six days after he signed the original promissory note, Sigman had signed it over to Clegg, to whom Sigman owed a debt of $13,000. This was done despite Sigman's verbal agreement with Dick that the note would not be assigned and would be renewed on an annual basis.

Meanwhile Sigman told David Early that he now wanted his shares signed back to him. "So we transferred the entire thing back to Sigman. I couldn't see any illegal aspects at the time," Early said. "Later, though, with the Paso Robles Inn padlocked and Sigman trying to scrape enough money to get Chalone for himself, the IRS went after him. And the IRS came to see me; they wanted to know what I knew. I knew nothing."

But Sigman did not keep his shares for long. He turned them over to another nominee, this time, Danforth Field. "Sigman told me it wasn't possible to own a winery and a business like the Paso Robles Inn at the same time," Field said. "Was it because of a liquor license? I don't know. I never did figure it out. Anyway, he turned his shares of the winery over to me. I was in the middle of things. One day John called and said, 'If we don't get $1,800 immediately, we're going to lose everything.' It was supposed to be for interest on Mrs. Graff's loan. I ended up paying it; I was the only one who had any cash." Field gave $1,800 to Sigman, but, according to Dick Graff, Sigman never gave $1,800 to Estelle Graff.

On May 29, 1968, Sigman traded the shares Field was holding for him plus Field's shares for a plot of land on the Monterey Peninsula. The trade was with Wilton DeMarco who wanted to be involved with the winery. Dick remembered that one day DeMarco appeared at Chalone in a white Cadillac. "He got out, looked around and said, 'So this is the place I own 47.5 percent of.' "

DeMarco's comment was true for only eight months. On February 2, 1969, DeMarco split his shares, giving half to his wife, Xenia, and half to Carl Outzen, a friend of Sigman whom DeMarco owed $8,000.

Danforth Field lost his patience. "I hired an attorney," he said, "and got my part back."

Meanwhile, Adrian Rose, Otto Clegg's lawyer, argued that Sigman was not in a position to give Dick a renewal of the promissory note. Charles Stewart, Dick's lawyer, having received promissory notes of $2,050 each from Estelle Graff and Darrell Corti for the shares he had sold to them, had in turn signed them over to the corporation as an offset against his promissory note for his shares.

Stewart and Rose each suggested a settlement for the amount of Sigman's debt to Clegg through new long-term notes. Ultimately, Clegg, understanding that Dick was in a difficult financial situation, returned the note to Sigman and demanded payment from him, rather than pursue Dick any further.

While Dick was trying to settle the problems with Clegg, he was also caught up in the more urgent entanglements with Sigman, Field and DeMarco. At the time, Chalone had no operating money, and Sigman would not provide any. But Chalone did have wine to sell—the 1966 vintage and the small vintage of 1967. Desperate for cash to continue the winery, Dick called his long-time friend, Louis "Bob" Trinchero of Sutter Home Winery in Napa Valley. Trinchero agreed to buy the entire inventory, and Dick moved all the wine up to Sutter Home.

When Sigman discovered the wine was gone, he and Field told their lawyer, Brian McGinty, to get a restraining order "to get Dick off the property because John said he shouldn't be there," Field said. When

McGinty tried to get such an order in March 1968, added Field, "We lost: We couldn't get a restraining order."

In the two and a half years after Dick received the first letter from Clegg's lawyer, Charles Stewart represented him and Conger Fawcett represented Estelle Graff in three intertwined lawsuits. Finally, Sigman and Field brought Dick to court. The case came to trial at the Superior Court of Salinas in July 1968. Dick was told that under the Parole Evidence Rule, verbal modifications of a written document are not binding. The terms of the promissory note had not been specific enough.

Dick realized that after nearly three years of fighting, he had lost Chalone.

"There was nothing I could do. I did not have the money to pay Sigman. And so my mother and I made a settlement. We would transfer our shares to Dan and Jennie Field, Xenia and Wilton DeMarco, and Sigman. Sigman and Field would take full possession of Chalone and pay Mother and me $5,000 each."

Estelle Graff, Charles Stewart and Dick returned to Chalone. They ate dinner quietly in the little house that Ed Liska had built. Dick thought about his time at Chalone and how more than anything else, he wanted Chalone. He also contemplated where he would go when he had to leave Chalone—perhaps to the Hall property that Bob Nikkel was holding for him.

It wasn't Chalone, but it was close by.

And then, in the tortuous route that has been Chalone's history, there was another sharp twist. Sigman's motive in suing Dick was to take over Chalone. Once he controlled the business, he told Field, he would sell it to an investor. The investor, however, asked his lawyer to look over Sigman's offer. After studying the plan, Field said, "the lawyer advised him not to touch it." Sigman was left with no buyer. Without a buyer, he could not pay $10,000 to the Graffs and, more important, he could not pay $25,000 for the deed of trust Estelle Graff held.

Suddenly, Dick's dream had new life. The deed of trust was a legal document very much like a mortgage; it was the first obligation on the property. In the three years she held it, Estelle Graff received no payment—interest or principal. And as the holder of a deed of trust, on which nothing had been paid, she had the right to foreclose on the property.

That is what Estelle Graff did. Following the procedure prescribed by the court, she first demanded payment from Jack Sigman. He ignored her demand. Legally, if the debtor, after receiving such a demand, does not make a payment in a given time, the entire amount becomes due and payable. If that is not paid, the owner of the deed of trust has the right to sell the property at auction.

Still, Jack Sigman did not pay. When Dick told Bob Nikkel about the situation, Nikkel said he would pledge $25,000 to buy Sigman out of the obligation. Dick made the offer to Sigman, who "disdainfully rejected it. I don't think he believed he would ever lose the property."

Finally, as the last step, Estelle went ahead with the public auction. By law, if no one bids more than the amount of the deed of trust, the property goes to the holder of the deed. If someone buys it for more than the amount of the deed, the bidder gets the property, the holder of the deed gets paid—in Estelle's case, $25,000—and the balance of the money goes to the person who owed the money—Sigman.

On February 18, 1969, Estelle Graff, Charles Stewart, Bob Nikkel and Dick Graff waited in the lobby of the Title Insurance and Trust company in Salinas for the auction to begin. With no money of his own, Dick once again prevailed on Bob Nikkel, and Nikkel agreed to bid on the property so that the Graffs would not lose it.

Other bidders gathered, too, as the auctioneer took his place. Just as he was about to open the bidding, a messenger rushed up and handed him a temporary restraining order. Carl Outzen had filed a complaint through his lawyer, Brian McGinty, on the grounds that he had offered to buy the note and deed of trust from Estelle Graff. In fact, McGinty had made an offer to her through Conger Fawcett, but it was made verbally, not in writing, in vague terms and included neither the intended buyer's name (Outzen) nor a check to confirm the offer. "The restraining order was given on flimsy grounds," Dick said, "but it was enough to postpone the auction for two weeks. The purpose behind the ploy was to give Sigman and Dan Field more time to find a buyer."

Two weeks later, on March 3, 1969, Estelle, Dick and Charles Stewart waited for the rescheduled auction to begin. But this time, Bob Nikkel was not there. He was in Europe.

"What am I going to do without you?" Dick had asked him.

"Don't worry," Nikkel assured him, "Nobody is going to bid on it."

"But there were plenty of people there ready to bid last time."

"Nobody is going to bid this time," Nikkel told him. "Mark my words. Nobody is going to bid."

He was right. Frightened away by Sigman's dramatic ploy two weeks earlier and by the implication that to win at the auction would be to plunge into litigation, no one appeared to bid. The auctioneer went through the proper procedure. "Who will bid?" he asked. No one answered.

And so, on March 3, 1969, almost five years after Dick Graff first saw Chalone, the slice of benchland that had become the home of his dreams had also become his mother's property.

7 | *A New Name and a Bright Future*

As a new era for Chalone began, Dick Graff wanted to draw a distinct line between it and the two previous companies that had used "Chalone" in their names, both to avoid confusion as well as to separate it from the prior companies' legal and tax problems. In June 1969, the corporation became Gavilan Vineyards, Inc.

"That was the official name of the corporation," said Conger Fawcett who became the new corporation's lawyer and secretary. "But, of course, we immediately made that a d.b.a.—doing business as—and continued to label the wines as Chalone Vineyard."

The new corporation gave Estelle Graff and Darrell Corti each 5 percent of the shares, comparable to what they had held in Chalone Vineyard, Ltd., and it bought the corporation from Estelle Graff for $65,000 with Dick keeping a lion's share of the stock. And Dick said, "We did it without using any of Bob Nikkel's money after all."

All of these developments made the vintage in 1969 an especially festive one. The grapes from the 1968 harvest had been sold. The 1969 harvest was to be the first under Dick's ownership, the first in which he would make and be responsible for all decisions. Again, family and friends came to help, and, this time, to celebrate as well. Nature, too, joined in with a glorious harvest. "Sixty-nine turned out to be a wonderful wine," Dick said.

With Dick in charge, Chalone truly became a family affair. His mother had been his staunchest supporter from the beginning, and other family members had helped out in the past during harvest. Now, they made trips to Chalone over the entire year. Estelle's older sister, Ninette Graff (she had married Dick's paternal grandfather after her first husband died) often came to Chalone on weekends. "I would stay in the little caretaker's house behind Dick's house," she said. "During the day, we'd bottle and label and cap. It was all handwork then; nothing was mechanized. We'd do maybe 10 cases a day. We worked hard and enjoyed it. I'd usually bring a friend so that in the evenings, we'd have four for bridge after dinner." Some weekends, Ninette's sons, Jonathan and Pete, also drove to Chalone to help. And Dick's brother Peter would come by as well.

Chalone remained primitive in the extreme. There was still no electricity, no telephone and no water line. All of the food had to be brought up from Soledad or Salinas, except for milk and eggs; they were bought on the benchland from Nettie Mathiesen.

Nettie Mathiesen was born in a sod house on the Great Plains in 1895 to a family of dirt farmers. She often told the story of receiving one orange as her sole Christmas gift, and how that was an amazing thing— an exotic token from a far land. She came to California in 1929, married Peter Mathiesen in the early 1940s and moved to the Gavilan benchland, where Peter had bought 320 acres adjacent to Chalone in 1939. While her husband built a house on the property, he, Nettie and Nettie's mother lived in a tiny two-room cottage that was little more than a shack. When the house was completed, he expected to move into it with Nettie and let his mother-in-law live in the tiny cottage. No, Nettie told him, her mother lives in the house with them. No, Peter Mathiesen told her, her mother lives in the cottage. If her mother doesn't live in the house, Nettie answered, neither does she. Her husband died in 1947. She continued to live in the cottage. Her mother died soon after. Nettie stayed in the cottage.

Peter Mathiesen left a son, Earl, and a daughter, Yvonne, by a previous marriage, as well as Nettie, but he did not leave a will. In deciding who should get the property, the judge gave each of them one third. The land Nettie was living on belonged to her. Still, she refused to move into the house. She remained in the cottage without electricity, without telephone, without an indoor bathroom for the more than 40 years that she lived on the benchland.

Nettie leased out some of her land to farmers who raised grain. On the rest of the land she maintained a cow named Daisy, chickens and a vegetable garden. Once a week, until she was too crippled with old age and arthritis, she would drive to Soledad to sell her eggs. Eventually she hired Jack Armbrister to help her around the property in exchange for room and board, despite the fact that she was a devout teetotaler and he was a devout alcoholic.

Most of the time Armbrister's love affair with Tokay did not interfere greatly with his work. He had done chores for Liska and Sigman both in the vineyard and in maintaining the buildings on their property. He had, in fact, stuccoed the outside of two of the buildings and roofed both the house that Liska built and the smaller caretaker's house.

But it was in the case of the roof, where Liska had given Armbrister money to buy nails, that Armbrister's love of Tokay did indeed leave its mark. Years later, on a windy Easter Sunday, as Dick and most of his maternal relatives gathered for the holiday dinner, the roof of the smaller house suddenly lifted up in the wind and sailed off. Ninette Graff's sons, both of whom were in the roofing business, were there, and discovered that Armbrister had used only six nails to hold the entire roof on to the rest of the building. Presumably, the rest of the nail money went toward another jug of Tokay.

The Easter dinner that was interrupted by the roof blowing off was prepared chiefly by Dick. "When I was growing up, " he noted, "it was a tradition in our family to have pancakes every Sunday. Since Mother hadn't learned to cook, my father would make them. Even as a little child, I would help him. Later I just took over the whole thing."

After he left the Navy in 1963, he bought "The Gourmet

Cookbook," a two-volume set that contained, he said, "the most complicated recipes you can imagine. But I figured that anyone who can read can learn to cook." Dick did more than learn to cook, he excelled. Thanks to the suggestion of his friend, Shirley Sarvis, a food writer in San Francisco, Dick wrote to Julia Child and invited her to Chalone. When she and her husband, Paul, visited in the 1970s, she proclaimed Chalone the first non-French wine she ever liked. Julia Child and Dick Graff were close friends from that point forward.

André Tchelistcheff visited Chalone with his wife Dorothy in the early 1970s. Some years ago, he remembered the occasion this way: "It was a summer evening. We were in Dick's tiny house, and he played the organ. He cooked dinner—he cooks artistically—the table was set with china and silver. I remembered it so well. Oh, it was beautiful," he said.

Tchelistcheff also remembered the wine Dick served that evening. It was the Chalone 1969 Pinot Noir. "Dick put a tremendous amount of effort and tears and blood into Chalone," he said. "I'm not going to say that I'm completely accepting his conclusion that the soil up there is exactly the same as the soil of Burgundy. Yes, the presence of lime is there, but the soils of Burgundy are [of] quite different geological origins. Physically, maybe they compare in some aspects, but Chalone and the Côte d'Or cannot parallel."

Still, it was wine made from Pinot Noir grapes grown in Chalone's soil that drew the highest praise from André Tchelistcheff. "When I tasted the 1969 on our visit, I knelt in front of Dick Graff. That happens not too often. It happened to me two or three times in Burgundy. In California, it happened only once, and that was at Chalone," he said.

And with that, a new day dawned over the remote Gavilan benchland—the home of Dick Graff's dream of producing truly Burgundian wines in California. Little did he know what a grand journey he had just begun.

8 | *The Beginnings of a Beautiful Partnership*

GROWING UP IN OTTAWA, ILLINOIS, PHILIP WOODWARD knew about only one wine—Asti Spumante—"because my mother had gone to school in Florence and she thought that was Italy's only wine. We had it every Christmas. For other occasions, my parents would drink Virginia Dare. Wine was definitely not part of our life."

In 1955, at the age of 15, Phil was sent east to school at Phillips Academy in Andover, Massachusetts. When he graduated three years later, he went west to the University of Colorado in Boulder, where he majored in history and economics. It was at the university that he met Diane McQuown, who, as it turned out, came from Sandwich, Illinois, about 30 miles from Phil's hometown. After earning his bachelor's degree, he went on to Northwestern University to study for his master's degree in business administration. In 1964 he received his MBA, and he and Diane were married.

"I had job offers to work in the Chicago area, which most people did if they went to Northwestern," Phil said. "But we (Diane and I) decided we wanted to make a break, so I ended up taking a job with Jones & Laughlin Steel Company in Pittsburgh. It took me about three months to realize that that was a mistake, at least a mistake from the standpoint of my career."

In spring of 1965, Phil answered a blind advertisement for a "consult-ant." The company turned out to be Touche Ross & Company, a large cpa/consulting firm with offices in most major cities. Phil was sent to Detroit, the company's largest office, where he was placed in a special training program for mbas. For two years, as part of the program, he worked with the audit staff. At the end of that time, having passed the exams, he was qualified as a cpa and assigned to the company's consult-ing staff.

"The reason I went to work for Touche Ross," Phil said, "was because my true interest was small business. If I went into banking, I could get a look-see into many different businesses but only from the view of a bank office. In public accounting, I would get the same opportunity but I would see these businesses in more depth. I would see people on site, and I would see how things really work. My hope was that eventually I would find a business I liked and would get involved with it as an owner."

Detroit turned out not to offer the small business opportunities Phil had hoped it would. But quite by chance, it offered a different kind of opportunity. Phil took his first wine appreciation course, offered in his office building by a faculty member of Wayne State University.

"It was a short course that covered everything from apéritifs to dessert wines, and it opened up a new world to me," Phil said. "I can even remember that the first wine on the first day was Cinzano Bianco. Of course, this was in the 1960s, when there weren't a whole lot of differ-ent wines from California to learn about, but there were two or three stores in the Detroit area where you could get wines like Beaulieu Private Reserve."

In two weeks, the course ended but Phil's interest was just beginning. He and Diane, who also had not grown up in a wine drinking family, started to buy wines and helped organize a wine club, meeting with friends once a month over dinner to taste. Each member took a turn to make a presentation on a particular wine type.

Meanwhile, after six years in Detroit, frustrated by the lack of small business activity there, Phil asked Touche Ross to transfer him. He was given a choice of five cities. When he saw that San Francisco was among the five, he hardly glanced at the other four names. Phil interviewed with the head of the San Francisco office at that time, Rick Kramer. "He told me years later that he was skeptical at first—he wasn't sure that I would fit in with the small business group he had put together," Phil said. But Kramer decided to take a chance on Phil and gave him a week to find a house and move to the Bay Area.

Phil arrived in San Francisco in November 1970. Within one week, he had bought a house. A lot of help in orienting himself in this new environment came from Diane's brother, John, who lived in the town of Mill Valley in Marin County.

"John McQuown—we call him 'Mac'—had a lot to do with introducing me to different wines while I was still in Detroit," Phil said. "So we already had that connection with him and when we were going to move out here, he said he thought Marin County was kind of a neat place to live. I told Diane that within a week I would find five houses that we could afford and then she'd fly out here, pick one, then go back, get the kids and we'd move. I can't imagine doing that today."

In January 1971, the house was ready for the family. By then, Diane and the two boys—Scott and Matthew—who were respectively about two months and two years old, moved to the bayside town of Belvedere in Marin County. Phil felt he could not be happier. "I thought not too many people get this opportunity—to have my family with our two little towheads, to live in this city, to have the work I always wanted and to be near wine country. My interest in wine was perking along, and by the time I moved to California, I thought I knew a bit."

He soon found he had been given one more opportunity—the chance to combine his new position at Touche Ross, as head of consulting for small businesses, with the budding West Coast wine industry. After only a few months in San Francisco, his consulting assignments included Touche Ross clients who were involved in Napa Valley wineries—Inglenook, which had recently been acquired by Connecticut-based spirits giant Heublein Inc., and the Seattle-based Rainier Brewing Company. Rainier at the time was co-owner of the then four-year-old Robert Mondavi Winery, and was looking for a way out of that investment. Phil's task was to help work on the negotiations that a few years later would allow Mondavi to buy out Rainier.

"For the first time I really saw the business side of what for me was a hobby that was fast getting out of control," Phil said. "I could see that you could make some money at this. I could see where Mondavi was headed, and so I thought, maybe this industry is where I could find something I really like and feel passionate about."

Shortly after his work with Rainier, Phil went to work with another Touche Ross client, Bud Van Loeben Sels, who was in the process of trying to raise money for what was then Oakville Vineyards.

"I did a lot of work for Bud. It was one of those things where they needed the credibility of Touche Ross to raise money, and he got me involved in just about anything I wanted to do in terms of putting together the prospectus and selling it," Phil said. Once again Phil saw what a business startup was like—the energy, the excitement. And he loved it.

"I probably worked on that account for a good year," said Phil. "Maybe it was six to nine months. In any case, it was quite a while, and Bud made me an offer to come and run it as president. I seriously considered it, but I really just felt that it wasn't the right time."

Little did Phil know that his decision to turn down the Oakville Vineyards job would lead him closer to the job he really wanted.

In early 1971 Phil began to do some consulting work to help a few small wine shops in San Francisco set up accounting and inventory control systems. Since this work was separate from his work at Touche Ross and since the shops could not afford to pay him money for these services, Phil asked that they pay him in wine. One day, having finished a small job for Esquin & Esquin Imports, they gave him a bottle of 1969 Chalone Pinot Blanc.

"Chalone—I've never heard of it," Phil said. "So I took this bottle home—I didn't even know there was a winery in Monterey—but I thought it was one of the best white wines I had ever had."

Phil went back to Esquin & Esquin and asked who had made the wine. "I'd like to meet this guy," Phil said. They told him, "His name is Dick Graff and you can't get a hold of him because there aren't any phones where he lives on the Chalone property." Chalone was somewhere in Monterey County, they said, but Graff could be reached in San Francisco once or twice a week—he was selling barrels for a company owned by Peter Newton, called Sterling Imports.

"So I called him," Phil said. "I told Dick that I would like to meet him and thought his wines were great. So we had lunch at the Tadich Grill in San Francisco. He brought the 1969 Chalone Chardonnay. That wine blew me away, too. I thought it was incredible."

Phil was inspired. He asked Dick if he would be willing to meet with his brother-in-law, John McQuown.

"Mac had been living in California since 1964, and whenever I visited him before I moved out West, we would drive north and go to wineries together. We both loved wine," Phil said. "At the time I met Dick, Mac was working at Wells Fargo Bank in the management services department. He agreed to meet with Dick but said he was very busy and could only stay a half hour. Well, if that's all the time you have, fine, I told him. Just bring your best bottle of white Burgundy."

The three men met for lunch in San Francisco at Julius' Castle restaurant on Telegraph Hill. Mac brought a 1966 Louis Latour Corton Charlemagne and Dick brought another bottle of the 1969 Chalone Chardonnay. First the half hour passed, then an hour, then another hour.

At the end of a three-hour lunch, Phil and Mac were thrilled with the Chardonnay and in awe of what Dick had told them about Chalone. "As much as we both loved wine," Phil said, "we never really thought we'd be able to get into the winemaking business." But listening to Dick, they were encouraged. Perhaps, after all, it just might be possible to be involved in some way."

Phil summed up his feelings about Dick Graff and that pivotal lunch:

"He knew a lot about the subject matter. He was obviously a smart guy and somebody who you just liked—you had to like this guy. But we never had any discussions about getting into business together. I knew what he was kind of doing. He was starting a little wine business from a property that his mother had bought at an auction. But Dick never really pushed it very hard, at least in the beginning. But we both liked Dick a lot."

"Mac and I had talked a lot about getting into the wine business, but we had pretty much decided we were never going to be able to do that. But after we met Dick and heard his story, we thought maybe we could at least own a vineyard." Phil and Mac thought they could buy one together in Napa Valley. They thought they could sell the grapes and maybe even build a second home there.

Phil and Mac had already looked at several vineyards in Napa Valley; none were quite right. They had also heard that Lee Stewart's Souverain property was for sale, so they drove up to take a look. "We went over the place and we thought it was great," Phil remembered. "But the problem was that there was a house on the property, and Lee Stewart wanted $100,000 for it and $300,000 for the rest. We didn't want the house, not at that price, and he wouldn't sell the property without it. So that deal fell through."

They looked at several other properties and had gotten to the point where they were almost ready to buy a property on Zinfandel Lane near St. Helena. "We thought we needed somebody else to take a look at it with us," Phil said. "So I said, 'Why don't I ask Dick? He would tell us.' So we did, and we brought Dick up to look at it and Dick gave us his opinion on the property."

At the end of that day, the three men stopped at a bar in St. Helena to talk and it was there that Dick made a suggestion to the discouraged Phil and Mac. "You know, if you guys are really interested in a vineyard, I have a property at Chalone that I don't own, but a friend of mine does. Maybe you'd be interested in buying that?"

The land Dick referred to was on the benchland—a 160-acre quarter section near Chalone. If Phil and Mac developed it, Dick promised them, he would buy their grapes. The land was the Hall property that Bob Nikkel had bought and agreed to hold until Dick could take it over. But it was clear that Dick would not be able to buy it. So, Phil and Mac decided to take a drive, visit Chalone and the Gavilan benchland, and see what Dick was so excited about.

"One night after work Mac and I drove down there, and for the first time we saw Chalone. We got there in the early evening. I remember because it was still light outside—we never would have found it otherwise," Phil said. "The first thing that struck me about the place was that it was really remote. I mean this place was so remote and so different than anything we had ever seen in terms of vineyards, we couldn't even believe it was there."

Dick was there with two other men—one was an investor, the other a friend. Dick made them all dinner and they talked about the Chalone story and plans for the future. Phil, while fascinated by the story was skeptical. "We got the story, but then you looked around. There was no water; there was no electricity—no utilities of any kind. You couldn't even have a phone," he said. "How could anyone live up here and really seriously think about having a business?" So, although they liked Dick and his wines a lot and decided to invest $1,000 each in Chalone, they still believed their destiny resided in a vineyard in the Napa Valley.

After that first visit, Phil and Mac drove to the benchland many times to go over the property. They looked at the almond orchard that was on it, at the house where no one had lived for 30 years, at the other old farm building. And for the next several months, they considered it.

During these months, Phil began to feel that perhaps his dream of being involved in a small business might be realized by Chalone. But he also felt that, unless Chalone raised a considerable amount of money, it was not going to last. It was clear that Dick, whom he felt he knew well by then and respected highly, was tremendously talented and dedicated. It also became clear that the business aspect of a winery was not the best place to put Dick's talent. But Phil felt it was the natural place for him.

Phil was also rethinking the "vineyard only" plan. "The more we looked at it in terms of what it was going to take to develop it, the amount of money and who was going to run it, the more we realized that this vineyard development thing could not stand on its own," Phil said. "You relied on the fact that you were going to sell the grapes to an entity that, frankly, had no money and no management. So that's when we began thinking that if we were going to do this, then maybe I should leave and be on both sides." In other words, Phil would be the General Partner of the new vineyard property along with Mac, while at the same time, work with Dick on the winery side to put together a viable company.

"If I could just find a way to keep going, to support my family while I got started in wine, I felt eventually the business could support us," Phil said. "By late 1971, I was sure that that was what I wanted to do."

Phil spoke to Dick. He told him he would quit his job—he could not continue to work for a public accounting firm and for Chalone at the same time—and would put all his efforts into raising money for Chalone and selling its wine. If Dick would agree to the idea, Phil would become Chalone's chief financial officer, Mac would be placed on Chalone's board of directors and, as soon as Phil left Touche Ross, he would also be on the board.

Dick agreed, and Phil set about making plans. He intended to leave his job in June 1972, which gave him a few months to cover all details and complete his current projects at Touche Ross. He was about to enter the wine business, and he was a happy man. And then he discovered another monumental event was to happen in June 1972. Diane was pregnant.

"I had to rethink everything," Phil said. "I had already borrowed money from my mother. I had taken a second mortgage on my house. I had taken the job at Chalone, and, at $500 a month, I could last five years. If at the end of five years it didn't work, if I hadn't turned Chalone around, I would be out of money. Now, with Diane pregnant, I thought, I cannot take the chance. I will not be able to go through with this. But Diane was wonderful. She supported me; she was with me. She knew how much I wanted this."

In June 1972, Diane gave birth to twin girls, Anne and Karen. That same month, Phil and Mac bought the 160-acre Hall ranch from Bob Nikkel for $50,000. Now, to develop their new benchland property, they created Macwood of Monterey (McQuown-Woodward) as a partnership. It began with three partners: Mac, Phil and Phil's mother. Two years later after Mac and Diane's father visited the benchland, he told his wife he, too, wanted to be part of it; six weeks later, before he had talked to Mac about it, he died. When Mac went home for the funeral, his mother told him about his father's wish. "He wanted to be a limited partner," she said. "Why can't I take his place?" And so the Macwood property became a partnership of Mac, Phil, their two mothers and the bank.

"We were going to plant vineyards and sell the grapes to Chalone," Phil said. "We were going to renovate the old house and have a weekend place. It seemed quite achievable—with the bank's help."

In August 1972, having delayed his plans only two months, Phil left Touche Ross and went to work for Chalone.

Very quickly, however, Phil and Mac began to have doubts about their plans for the Macwood property. Chalone was in such poor financial condition; how would it pay for their grapes? And even if it could eventually pay, how would they make enough money to manage their loans on the property? Profits in the wine business, they soon realized, came from wine, not grapes. Perhaps what they ought to do, he reasoned, was to buy a bigger piece of Chalone itself. In September 1972, Phil and Mac each bought another 1,000 shares at $20 a share. Meanwhile, to augment his salary from Chalone, Phil took a part-time job with one of his former clients. For one year, he would work nights and weekends as a consultant on mergers and acquisitions.

"I couldn't afford to only do Chalone," Phil said. "So one of my former Touche Ross clients, Bob Green, gave me the ability to work for him for a whole year to find acquisitions. At the time, he was CEO of Community Psychiatric Centers, which he had taken public. He agreed to pay me the same thing that I was making at Touche Ross for a whole year."

With Phil now working full time, Chalone needed an office in San

Francisco. And Phil's first coup was to get one at 655 Sutter Street. It was tiny and in the basement but the rent was right—it was free. The building was owned by Jerry Draper, who also owned the Esquin & Esquin wine shop and import business where Phil had first heard of Chalone. Draper planned to renovate the building, move the wine shop in and rename the property the Vintners Building. Chalone became his first tenant.

"The office was just big enough to hold two desks and a telephone," Phil recalled. "That was our office for the first year; after that, when the renovation was complete, we were to move to the second floor and pay rent. That's how we began. I was selling what little wine we had. I was raising money, keeping the books, and answering the phone—although it didn't ring very much. I needed someone to work with me, so I asked my sister Wendy who had just graduated from the University of California at Berkeley if she would help temporarily until I could find someone to take her place." She stayed 23 years.

Phil worked hard to get Chalone's wine into the city's restaurants and retail shops. Mostly, he worked hard to raise money. With Mac's help, as well as that of Conger Fawcett, Chalone's attorney, he was able to sell $200,000 worth of shares. Chalone had never seen that kind of money.

"Conger Fawcett helped us put together all the things legally, and there were certain restrictions on what you could do, but essentially what I did was just follow any lead I could," Phil said. "Mac knew a lot of people, Dick knew people, I knew some. Most of the people were clients of Touche Ross who I knew had an interest in wine, and so we went to them with this idea. What made it a little bit easier than a startup was that Dick actually had wine he had made in 1969 that was outstanding. The 1970 vintage was good; the '71 vintage was very good. The point is that we did have some wines to taste and a brand name to show people who had an interest in investing in a winery.

"The fact that we were so remote and so completely out of the mainstream didn't seem to make a whole lot of difference to most people. If they really cared about wines and they wanted to be a part of a wine company, I went anywhere they would listen to me," Phil said. "We had

New York investors, we had Texas investors, and usually they would be professionals who had the money and discretionary income and a love for wine. They wanted to be involved and looked at it as a long-term investment."

That's not to say this period wasn't filled with its share of sleepless nights for Phil Woodward. He had just made a "cold turkey" career jump from a comfortable role as a consultant with a huge national firm to an entrepreneur in an undercapitalized, labor- and capital-intensive business. How did he cope?

"The best thing I had to fall back on was all the experience I got at Touche Ross in the accounting and tax areas; this time probably gave me more of the tools to work with than anything else. At least I felt I knew where to start," Phil said. "But it was a total culture shock. In those days I did everything from delivering the wine to selling the stock."

But he had to admit to himself that it felt good. No, it felt great!

And at the end of the first year with Chalone, Phil's part-time job ended as planned and, he said, he learned to live on less money than he ever thought possible.

WHEN PHIL AND MAC BOUGHT THEIR MACWOOD PROPERTY, they had planned to develop 100 acres in vineyards. The first 24 acres were planted in 1972, followed by 26 acres more in 1973 and 20 acres in 1974. After that, they stopped for a while; they were out of money and did not want to borrow more. The Macwood company, after all, consisted only of the two brothers-in-law and their mothers.

The 1972 harvest, the first for Phil, was one of the winery's worst. He, Dick and Dick's brother, John Graff, worked hard, but again, the birds had pecked open and eaten most of the grapes. "We never even labeled the 1972 Pinot Noir," Phil said, "and most of our white wine that year was not very good. I saw that there would not be much of anything to sell, and I realized we were going to have to raise more money just to stay afloat. And that's what I did. I sold more stock in the corporation."

That vintage—what there was of it—was made where all Chalone's wines had been made, in the tiny winery Philip Togni had created out of Will Silvear's chicken coop. It was wildly primitive, romantic, challenging. But if Chalone was going to develop into a viable, competitive winery, Phil decided, it would need a modern winery. That, of course, meant that he would need to raise still more money. And he did.

"Mac and I had a friend, Roland Masse in Marin, who built houses," Phil said. "So we asked him if he would build a winery for us. He came down to Chalone and said, 'How am I going to build a winery where there's no electricity?' But he knew us and so he said he would do it.

"The first thing he did was to move down to Chalone. He moved down there into a trailer. He then built the winery by using generators. He had one guy who moved down, too, and worked with him. He and Dick designed the winery, and then Roland put it on paper, got the permits, and he and Dick built it together. Dick went down and got his electrical union license, got his plumbing license, and did all the plumbing and electrical," Phil said.

They labored through 1973 and much of 1974, finishing just in time for that year's harvest. The new building was large enough to handle 12,000 cases of wine.

"If we could make that much wine and I could sell it for about $10, $12 a bottle," Phil reasoned, "we'd have no problems. We would all be able to make a nice living." Up to then, Chalone had been making about 2,000 cases a year—almost.

The last vintage made in the chicken coop winery was 1973, and it was a wonderful vintage, a fine and fitting farewell to the past and Phil's first try at working the harvest. The first vintage in the new winery, in 1974, was not only equally good in quality, it was also the largest crop Chalone ever had. The old winery could never have handled it.

Now that Chalone was a corporation, it had to hold annual meetings. The first, in 1973, was held in Dick's little house. There were six people present and the meeting lasted 10 minutes; afterward, they drank wine and talked about what they would like to accomplish in the coming year.

By the time the next annual meeting was held, Phil had sold considerably more stock, and about 25 people were expected—far too many for Dick's house. It was held instead in the A-frame house that Phil and Mac had just completed on the Macwood property. After the business roundup, food and wine were served.

At the 1975 meeting, almost 50 people came, some in campers and others with sleeping bags; later, a catered lunch accompanied the wines. It was a meeting, but it was also a party.

Later, Phil Woodward took stock of his progress. He was three years into his five-year plan. The 1972 harvest was a disaster, but 1973, 1974 and now 1975 were fabulous vintages. Things were going just as he had planned.

"They were heady years—1973, 1974, 1975. We were getting shareholders. We were getting money. We had three good vintages. We were right on track." He was going to make it after all.

9 | *Have Wine, Will Deliver*

THROUGH THE 1975 HARVEST, Chalone's future was promising. And as he steered the corporation through its growth and managed its financial health, Phil Woodward felt both he and the winery "were right on track."

That's not to say that things were easy, however. Raising money for the company was one thing, but selling wine on the streets for the fledgling company was sometimes quite another thing entirely.

"Selling the wines in California was a hell of a lot easier than selling outside of California," Phil said. "We could probably sell everything we had to our mailing list, but I felt we needed to get out into the stores and some restaurants. Because the 1969 vintage actually got some really nice reviews—Robert Lawrence Balzer had written it up in the *Los Angeles Times* and it was chosen to be at the San Francisco Food and Wine Society dinner one year—I saw an opportunity to broaden our horizons."

Phil began to slowly build his network of wine retailers and restaurants, while at the same time building the company's list of mail-order customers. Not only did he personally visit each prospective retail and restaurant account, but initially he even delivered the wines personally.

"I'd deliver the wines on Saturdays not only to stores we had, but I'd also deliver the wines to the mailing list people," Phil said. "I'd go to all their houses in this van. I'd take my oldest boy, Scott, with me. At the time he must have been about five, today he's one of our National Sales Managers. So, we'd go around to these people's homes and they, for the most part, had no clue who I was. I remember one of the stores in the East Bay was frequented by friends of ours who lived over there. They used to come down to Chalone and help us with the harvest. Well, they came down to help us one time and she told me the story that she went in to this store and told the owner there that they were friends of the Woodwards. The guy said, 'Yeah, I know who he is. He's the delivery guy.' "

Selling the wines outside of California was not so easy. While the 1969 vintage had been such a success, and the 1970 and 1971 good but not as good as '69, Phil's efforts outside California were sometimes met with a less than enthusiastic response. "It was a whole different story," Phil recalled. "Some of the early states that I took on, like Illinois and Texas and even New York, first of all, weren't all that wild about California wines. Second, the concept of a wine from Monterey was so strange to them that many said, 'What do I want with another white wine from California, let alone Monterey?' I went to four or five distributors in Chicago and three or four in Texas and was getting turned down left and right all the time."

Then, as often happens, Mother Nature threw a king-sized monkey wrench into the works. The two-year drought of 1976 and 1977 caught most of California completely unprepared. Nearly non-existent rainfall across the state caused widespread hardship for the state's population as well as business and agricultural interests. Chalone with its total depend-ence on rainfall and run-off from the surrounding hills was particularly hard hit.

"1976 was the first year of the drought, and, frankly, I never dreamed it was going to be as bad as it was," Phil remembered. "By the time 1977 was here, it was clear there wasn't going to be any rain. We had to do something. We had to raise money to keep things going. I remember ask-ing myself over and over how we were going to do it."

Phil could see that with a serious drought, already small yields at

Chalone would be down significantly and there was no way the company could survive on the wine produced from Chalone's grapes alone. The drought forced Phil and Dick to make some decisions about growth and diversification well before they were really ready to do so.

Phil knew that he needed to find ways to generate additional sales revenue to make up for the lost Chalone sales. The first idea was to find a new wine he could sell in addition to the regular Chalone lineup—one that did not depend on Chalone for grapes.

In 1974 Chalone had begun to bottle French Colombard from the Cyril Saviez Vineyard near Calistoga under the Chalone label. "We wanted an everyday white wine," Phil said. "The Colombard was pretty different from any other Colombard on the market. It was bigger and more complex from being barrel fermented. We all felt it was pretty good. At the time, we weren't making very much of it, but we knew that it sold." So, phase one of the Chalone drought survival strategy became an expanded French Colombard program.

What Phil didn't count on was that Cyril Saviez wouldn't want to sell Chalone more of his grapes. "Trying to buy grapes in Napa was impossible," Phil said. "First of all, they didn't have any to sell, and second they sure weren't going to sell them to someone from Monterey." Phil went up to meet with Cyril about buying more of the Colombard grapes. Cyril's response was, "I'll sell to the Mondavis and they'll pay me a good price. Why should I sell to you?" Phil's response was to propose that Cyril's name appear on the wine's label. According to Phil, "All of a sudden, that changed everything. Cyril said, 'Well, that's not a bad idea. Cyril Saviez Vineyard.' After that, he gave us all of his French Colombard."

Securing the grape source for the Colombard was only part of the challenge to come with that wine. The grapes had to be picked in Calistoga and then transported down to Chalone. Again, Phil took to driving the delivery truck. "I drove a U-Haul truck up to Calistoga to get the boxes of grapes, load the truck and then drive it back down to Chalone. I'd get down there at night and unload it in the morning. Then I'd drive back up again to get the next load," Phil said.

The second answer to the drought came during a board meeting. What about doing private label wines? Chalone, with its new 12,000-case capacity, had the space. "If we could make wine for other people, put their brand name and 'Produced and Bottled by Chalone' on the label, it would be a unique kind of marketing," Phil reasoned. "And we could collect money for it up front, which we needed." It was an idea worth trying, the board felt, if Phil could find the customers and the grapes.

"We had to figure out some way that we could sell wine quickly, get money quickly and not divert from our strategy of having Chalone as an estate bottled winery," Phil said. A private label program seemed the perfect solution.

So Phil scoured the state looking for grapes. With the drought, supplies were very slim and echoing Cyril Saviez' initial reaction, people in Napa and Sonoma scoffed at the idea of selling grapes to a "Monterey" winery.

It was through Chalone's bank, Wells Fargo, that Dick and Phil first heard about Paragon Vineyards in the Edna Valley near San Luis Obispo. Wells Fargo had financed the startup of the operation for the Niven family and 1976 was to be their first crop. Even more interesting to Dick and Phil, the grapes were Chardonnay and Pinot Noir.

"So we, through the bank, got to know who the Nivens were and went down to see what they were doing," Phil said. "They had sold some grapes to Mike Grgich when he was at Chateau Montelena during that period. Here was somebody ready to give us all the Chardonnay we wanted and Dick thought everything looked good. So we made the first private label wine in 1977 from Edna Valley grapes."

Next, it was Phil's job to find people who wanted to buy private-label wine from Chalone. He contacted some of Chalone's better customers in the state and managed to line up six private label accounts that year: wine retailers John Walker & Company in San Francisco; Wally's, Duke of Bourbon, and Red Carpet Liquors in Los Angeles; and Le Central and Perry's, restaurants in San Francisco.

"We asked for half the money in advance as a commitment. That's how we financed it," Phil said. "When the grapes were ripe, we brought them up to Chalone, made the wine and then bottled and labeled them with these private labels for each account. The wine turned out to be really good, so good that we did private labeling again in 1978. We got such raves about the 1978 wines that we knew we had something good going." But Phil didn't just mean the private label program. He and Dick realized that they liked the Niven family, and they liked the quality of their grapes.

Jack Niven, the family patriarch, had been the president and major owner of the Purity Stores grocery chain until he liquidated that business, took the proceeds and bought a lot of acreage in the Edna Valley area southeast of San Luis Obispo. At the time there were not many vineyards in the area, so he consulted the professors at UC-Davis as to which varieties he should plant. Fortunately for Dick and Phil, two of the varieties that Jack planted in his Paragon Vineyard were Chardonnay and Pinot Noir.

By 1979 it was clear that not only was the private label program working, it was thriving. So Phil began to talk to Jack Niven about doing something more. "We started to think joint venture," Phil said. "We had no money, and they did. But they didn't know how to make wine or sell it. We did."

Phil's idea was to have Chalone build a winery in Edna Valley with Niven's Paragon Vineyards as a partner. "After about 25 lunches with Jack, we negotiated a deal that was to become Edna Valley Vineyard," Phil said. "Paragon would provide the grapes and build a winery. Chalone would make the wine, sell it and run the business. Chalone and Paragon would each own 50 percent of the venture." Edna Valley Vineyard became a legal entity that would pay Paragon for the grapes, which in turn would be used to pay Paragon's payments on the winery. Profits of the business would be divided 50-50. And the beauty of it from Phil's perspective was that Chalone had to put very little money in.

"Jack was a sharp businessman—very low key," Phil said. "He was somebody who you could trust. So, when we had all these discussions, we could do it without having our attorneys there. He had a great sense of humor, and he really wanted to have this large vineyard business. He felt that would be a good investment for his family, so they all moved and built a house in Edna Valley."

Like the Chalone benchland, Edna Valley poses challenges for growing grapes. The cooler climate and the significant coastal influence in the form of breezes and coastal fog can make each harvest a challenge. "Even Chardonnay is tough because it can get really cool for a long period of time. We'd harvest the Chardonnay there a good month after we did it at Chalone, if not six weeks."

But Phil and Dick knew about adversity and winemaking under less than ideal conditions. Everything about the Edna Valley venture made it look like a perfect fit. "We realized how good this could be," Phil said. "It was the next step in what Dick and I had always talked about—several wineries under a Burgundian-style wine company umbrella."

The new winery at Edna Valley was designed to produce 25,000 cases, compared to Chalone's 12,000-case capacity—plenty to get the new company back on the growth track. The new label even resembled the Chalone label and tied the two wines together in the marketplace. "A lot of people thought that it was Chalone's second label, which it wasn't," Phil said. "The idea was to make it a lower-priced wine in the same winemaking style as Chalone, but obviously from an appellation that had an identity of its own." Phil and Dick settled in to build their new brand and their new partnership with the Nivens slowly and deliberately.

The drought-year harvests were not good in quantity or quality, and the 1977 whites were particularly poor. However, the years following the drought were good years on the benchland. The 1978 wines were so outstanding, in fact, that it was decided to separate some of the best barrels of Chardonnay and hold them as reserve wines. By the late 1970s, Chalone had many new shareholders due to Phil's fund-raising efforts. To offer them a special wine not available to the general public, Chalone labeled the bottles "Shareholder's Reserve" and sold them only to those people who were indeed shareholders of Chalone. It was the first reserve

Chalone had ever made.

No reserve wine was made in 1979. In 1980, another wonderful vintage, the winery began a regular reserve program. It included Pinot Noir, Chardonnay and Pinot Blanc produced from older vines that produced a wine with more concentrated and complex flavors.

DICK'S BARREL IMPORTING BUSINESS, which began with Siruge barrels from Burgundy, expanded rapidly. Soon he was handling barrels from Demptos in Bordeaux as well as barrels from Italy and Germany.

About that time, Sterling International was building Sterling Vineyards in Napa Valley, and the company asked Dick to consult on the project. Together with Ric Forman, who was to be winemaker, and Martin Waterfield, an executive with Sterling International, Dick helped to design and plan the winery. Through this assignment, he met Peter Newton, then president of Sterling International.

When Bob Nikkel, who had backed Dick's barrel business, said he would now like to be out of it, Dick spoke to Peter Newton. It was agreed that Sterling International would go into the barrel business with Dick and would provide letters of credit and an office. With that, the barrel business' name changed from Worldwide Import-Export Company to Winery Equipment Import Company. Under its new co-ownership, it lived up to its name, expanding to include not only barrels but also corkers, filters, bottling lines, crusher-stemmers and other winery equipment.

By 1974, however, as Chalone demanded more and more of his time, Dick left the barrel business entirely to concentrate on the winery. He did, however, continue his involvement with Mount Eden, where his brother Peter was winemaker. When Peter left to work at Chalone, Dick hired Merry Edwards, a new Davis graduate, and supervised winemaking while she was there. When Edwards left after a couple of vintages, Dick once again had to take over as winemaker until a replacement could be hired.

Then, in 1979, Chalone was asked to completely take over the management of Mount Eden, and for the next three years, Phil and Dick operated it together with a winemaker and an assistant.

Dick's brother John Graff was an early convert to Chalone. "I first came here in 1966. At that time, the road from Soledad to here was 10 miles of dirt, and I got lost," John said. "I couldn't believe there was anything out there, no less a vineyard. I might never have made it that day if Dick didn't come down to see what happened to me and found me on the road. I did some work for him; then I left for the University of Chicago for six years."

In 1972, having earned his doctorate in chemistry, John took some time off to travel. Eventually, his travels led him to Chalone, and when Dick said he needed help with the harvest, John set to work. "I figured it would be for a short time. But what happened is that I fell in love with the place. It's hard to communicate this feeling—some people come here and understand it, some don't—but for me, Chalone is magic. And so I didn't leave after harvest. I stayed on for six years."

John Graff worked at Chalone form 1972 to 1978. For four of those years, he lived on the benchland with his daughter, Lisa, who was nine years old when they arrived. Each morning during the school year, John drove her down to Soledad, and each afternoon, he picked her up. They lived in the caretaker's house.

"There were very few people up here," John said. "My brother Peter and his wife Deborah moved here in 1974. There were Nettie Mathiesen and Jack Armbrister. I would shovel out Nettie's chicken coop when it needed shoveling and Jack was off drunk somewhere. And there was a couple, George and Betty Creal. They had bought part of the Gummow property that lay between Chalone and Macwood in 1968. They were from the Midwest and were raising cattle.

John helped to plant the Macwood vineyard and put in new vineyards at Chalone. He also helped to build the new winery. And he helped to make wine each fall. "During harvest time, I'd average 84 hours a week," John said. "I kept track of the time, and it was more than 12 hours a day, no days off, for two months. For the first couple of years, it was exciting. All I could think of was that I was making wine. After a few harvests, though, I would remember how hard the work was and think, I've got to do that again?

Lisa did not like Soledad but she loved Chalone. So did John. And although it was quiet and lonely during the week, on many weekends, John's mother, Estelle Graff, his Aunt Ninette and friends would come to Chalone to work. Still, at times, the solitude of the place overwhelmed both its beauty and magic. In 1978, John was remarried, to Rosemary, and he left Chalone to live with her in Santa Barbara.

Dick's youngest brother, Peter, had helped at Chalone occasionally, and like so many others, he was beguiled by its wild remoteness. During his junior year in college in Southern California, he transferred to UC-Davis to major in chemistry. He soon discovered, he said, that chemistry was beyond him, and he switched to enology and viticulture. Between starting and finishing his new major, however, he took a detour, leaving school to work with rock and roll bands as "credit manager, stand-in drummer, security guard, whatever they needed. I was young."

Eventually, he "got tired of starving" and, since Dick needed somebody to help him, came to work at Chalone for a while in 1971. From there Peter returned to Davis, graduated in 1972 and went to work for Hanzell Vineyard in Sonoma. Six months later, Dick asked him to work as vineyard manager and winemaker at Mount Eden, under Dick's direction until early 1974. By then Chalone was building its new winery and planting new vineyards. Peter was needed. In the spring of that year, he and his wife, Deborah, moved to Chalone and Peter became vineyard manager.

They had planned to live in the old house on the Macwood property, but the carpenters working on the new winery were housed there. So, for a few months, until the house was available, Peter and Deborah pitched a teepee on the ground for their bedroom and shared the kitchen in the little house where John and Lisa lived.

"The teepee was uncomfortable for Deborah, especially since she was pregnant," Peter said. In fact, life at Chalone was uncomfortable for her. After the new winery was finished and the carpenters left, they were able to move into the old house on the Macwood property. "It was in such bad condition, we named it Stomach Acres. It was so isolated up here—no electricity, no telephone. When the baby was due, we went to Petaluma. We wanted natural childbirth, and there was a midwife there to help."

After their son Kevin was born, Peter and Deborah returned to Chalone, but life on the benchland was still difficult. "Deborah is a city girl, not a country person, and I sort of tricked her into moving down here. There were so few people. We were 10 miles from nowhere, because we were 10 miles from Soledad and Soledad was nowhere," Peter said.

After John left Chalone in 1978, Peter became winemaker, and a vineyard manager named Coby Bryant was hired to replace him. But life at Chalone never became easier for Peter's wife. When Kevin reached school age, Deborah moved away with him to the Monterey Peninsula.

In 1979 Chalone hired Michael Michaud. A recent graduate of UC-Davis, where he majored in chemistry and studied enology and viticulture as well, Michaud was appointed assistant winemaker; Peter was named general manager.

In his new position, Peter was sent to the Monterey Institute to learn French; and because of the winery's interest in Pinot Noir and Chardonnay, he was then sent to Burgundy to study winemaking methods there. In 1983 he returned to Burgundy for two months. Soon after he returned, he left Chalone. He took a year off to be a househusband, and when he felt his marriage strong again, he took a job at another winery.

When Peter left Chalone, Michael Michaud was promoted to winemaker, a position he would hold until 1997.

❧

THE MACWOOD PROPERTY WAS SEPARATED from Chalone by 320 acres. They were acres that Phil felt Chalone should have. The problem was that George Creal, who had owned them since 1968, did not want to sell them. Creal used some of his land for cattle, "but for the most part," Phil said, "he lived on his railroad pension, smoked cigarettes constantly and drank the strongest coffee I've ever tasted in my life. Dick had tried over and over to get him to sell the property to us, but all George would say is no, no, no."

It wasn't that Creal had any animosity toward Chalone. On the contrary, Conger Fawcett commented, "George was very supportive of everything Phil and Dick did. And he always used to say to them, 'I feel some day you boys ought to have my property.'" But that day had not yet come.

"So it was now my job," Phil continued, "to get him to change his mind. Each weekend when I was at Chalone, I'd go over to see him. I'd sit there struggling to drink that bad coffee. Then I'd ask him to sell the property to us, and all he would say is no, no, no."

Then one weekend, when Phil was driving his van down the Pinnacles road and George Creal was driving up in his beat-up old truck, Creal motioned to Phil to stop. He poked his head out the window and said to Phil, "You still want to buy my property?"

"Yes, George, we still do."

"Well, why don't you come over and let's write it down."

Phil went over. "I thought, for this, I'm willing to get through one more cup of coffee." Creal took out a piece of paper. "This is what I want," he said. "I want $59,000. I want it in cash, no financing. And I want to keep living here for a while."

Having Creal live there a while was not a problem; the $59,000 was. "We couldn't afford it," Phil said. "We could only afford to buy 160 acres. I had to find someone else to buy the other 160 acres with the promise to sell it back to us at a later date when we could afford to buy it."

On June 11, 1974, Gavilan Vineyards bought the lower part of Creal's property for $27,000. The following year, on September 25, 1975, Jack Chambers bought the upper part of the Creal property for $32,000. Later Chambers and his wife, Barbara, renamed the property Domaine St. Jacques and brought in other partners. Eventually, in 1982, they sold it back to Gavilan Vineyards.

The 1970s came to an end at Gavilan Vineyards, Inc. in 1979 with another promising development: the company's first profit. With all the struggles and hard work of the last seven years fresh in all of their minds, as well as the hard work ahead of them, the accountant in Phil Woodward had to smile.

*The Pinnacles as
they overlook the
Chalone Vineyard*

*The old "chicken coop"
– the first winery
at Chalone*

*Current Chalone
winemaker Don Karlsen*

Aerial view of the winery at Chalone Vineyard

Phil Woodward and Dick Graff talk with shareholders at the annual shareholder celebration

Phil Woodward relaxes at the annual shareholder celebration

Early photo of
Phil Woodward
in Chalone's
San Francisco offices

Dick Graff holding a bottle
of Chalone Chardonnay

The winery at
Edna Valley Vineyard

97

*Vineyards at Edna Valley
with ancient dormant
volcanoes in background*

*The Carmenet winery
nestled up against the
Mayacamas Mountains*

*Mike Richmond
and Jeff Baker*

*The Acacia winery
in Carneros*

*Acacia's founding
winemaker Larry Brooks*

*Canoe Ridge winemaker
John Abbott*

Snow at Canoe Ridge Vineyard

Baron Eric de Rothschild
of Domaines Barons
de Rothschild (Lafite)

Tom Selfridge, president
and CEO of Chalone
Wine Group

*Christophe Salin,
president of DBR*

*Preparing a course
for diners at the
annual celebration*

*Chalone employees
deliver the lunch at
the annual celebration*

101

*Shucking oysters
for more than
1,000 shareholders*

*Some of the thousands
of wine glasses used at the
annual celebration*

*Dick Graff escorts
Julia Child to the shareholder
celebration at Chalone*

PART THREE

❧

The Modern Company
Emerges

10 | *An Idea Begins to Form*

DICK GRAFF AND PHIL WOODWARD began the 1980s with a pause to consider how far they had come.

The corporation now owned Chalone and half of Edna Valley. And that fit neatly into the overall philosophy that Phil and Dick had agreed upon since their early days as partners. That philosophy was based on the premise of improving Chalone, honing it as near to perfection as a winery and its wine could be and allowing it to grow only to a given size. More growth would come by creating or buying new small wineries that fit with Chalone's Burgundian style.

"The original idea was to make Chardonnay and Pinot Noir and a little bit of Pinot Blanc, obviously, but from different regions in California under different brand names, and all under the Chalone umbrella," Phil said.

"We wanted always to have a quality at Chalone that distinguished it from all other wines," Phil said. "Dick shared this theory of quality, and it showed in everything he did—from the kinds of barrels to the bottles and corks he used. He did things nobody else was doing in those days. So, when we looked to expand, we looked to essentially recreate the Chalone concept on a larger scale at a new winery in a different appellation."

Edna Valley was that winery. It produced the same types of wine—Chardonnay and Pinot Noir—but because these wines sold at lower prices, they did not compete with Chalone. In 1980, the Edna Valley winery was completed and ready for that year's harvest, and the company was ready to grow.

With two wineries to oversee now, Dick decided the shortest distance between them would be by air. In 1980 he earned his private pilot's license and, in the following year, had a 1,750-foot-long landing strip prepared at Chalone. Dick, in his single-engine Cessna 182 Skylane, commuted between winery, vineyard and offices.

BY 1980 NETTIE MATHIESEN, CHALONE'S NEIGHBOR on the benchland, was severely crippled with arthritis. Jack Armbrister had died in the late 1970s, and so Earl and Clarice Mathiesen, Nettie's stepson and his wife, would drive up the valley a couple of times a week to care for her. A year later, she moved to Bakersfield. In her will, she left her third of the benchland property to eight relatives—her sister Anna, and her nieces and nephews.

Nettie's third plus the two thirds left to Earl Mathiesen and his sister Yvonne totaled 320 acres, about 200 acres of it running from Chalone's boundary to Highway 146, with the remaining acreage continuing on the other side of the highway.

Phil and Dick were eager to buy that land, and Dick offered $500 per acre for it. Earl Mathiesen, who was handling the sale, wanted twice that much. He sold it at that price to Richard Peterson (a well-known California winemaker who is now co-owner of Folie à Deux in St. Helena) and Martin Crowley, who wanted to establish vineyards and a winery there in competition with Chalone. When their plans failed and the property went into foreclosure, Mathiesen bought it back. By then, Phil and Dick really didn't want to miss another chance to acquire the land, so Chalone bought it for Mathiesen's asking price—$1,000 an acre.

While Chalone bought the entire 320 acres, Phil and Dick really wanted only the part that was on their side of the highway; the other side, they reasoned, would be a bit awkward to farm. What to do with the other 120 acres?

It would take eight years for Phil to find the answer to that question. He did, however, find it close to home in Dick's three brothers. David, the principal investor, and John and Peter bought the parcel in 1988. The brothers moved slowly, planting mainly Rhône varietals Syrah and Mourvèdre, as well as Pinot Blanc. Much later, the wine made from these grapes, combined with those from Dick's original vineyard, would be bottled under the "Graff Family Vineyards" label and sold by the Chalone Wine Foundation.

TRAGEDY STRUCK CHALONE and its partners on January 30, 1981, in the form of a fire that gutted the "A-Frame"—the house that Macwood partners Phil Woodward and John McQuown had built on a small corner of their property and used for eight years as the site of the company's annual meeting and celebration.

"The A-frame was built because my brother-in-law, Mac McQuown, and I wanted a place to stay when we went down to Chalone," Phil said. "There was a little 3.5-acre piece that was cut off at the very corner of the property because of Stonewall Canyon Road. So we thought, 'Well, we're never going to develop that into grapes, so why not use that as our house site?' It also was nice because it was up high. So we built an A-frame house on that piece. We actually put it into a different partnership so that it would be separate from Macwood, since we knew we would eventually sell Macwood to the company.

"The A-frame was built in 1973. It was a double A-frame with a great wine cellar underneath. We also planted some Cabernet Sauvignon grapes that we eventually made into the A-Frame Cabernet. So it was just built as a place to hang out with the family and the kids, and then it became a place for the receptions after the annual meetings.

"The house burned in January 1981. It was arson—they burned it to cover up a burglary. Several years later, the sheriff actually caught the perpetrators.

"From time to time, people would come up the hill from Soledad just to look around. These guys must have seen the house and figured there would be something to steal. There really wasn't anything to steal; they took few things—personal things of mine—and that's how we caught them, because the girlfriend remembered the items. They took those to the flea markets the next day. They realized that they had left their fingerprints behind and that they were wanted for all these other crimes. So they figured the only way to get rid of the fingerprints was to burn down the house. So they doused gasoline all over the place, lit a match, and up it went," Phil said.

The fire burned so hotly that it just simply burned everything to ashes. It burned through the floor and into the wine cellar, where approximately 100 cases of wine were stored. All the bottles burst and the wine ran down the cellar's floor drain. The next morning as Phil drove up to the scene, he was greeted with the sight of red wine flowing down the driveway from the drain.

Investigators initially suspected Phil of setting the fire. Phil and Diane, on the night of the fire, had had dinner in Tiburon near San Francisco. Investigators reasoned that he had had time to leave dinner, drive to Chalone, set the fire and then return to Tiburon. His motive allegedly was to obtain the insurance proceeds.

II | *An Opportunity or a Distraction?*

WHILE DICK AND PHIL WORKED HARD to finish the new winery at Edna Valley and to keep Chalone on track, developments taking place more than 200 miles to the north would soon become a pressing part of their daily lives.

John McQuown, Phil's brother-in-law, and four other investors had located a property high up on the western slopes of the Mayacamas Mountains—the range that separates the Sonoma and Napa valleys. This property, on the remote eastern edge of the Sonoma Valley, was named Glen Ellen Vineyard after the small town situated about five miles to the west, down in the heart of the valley.

At the end of Moon Mountain Road, the Glen Ellen Vineyard property had a long history of grape growing, going back 100 years or more. The area was originally planted before the turn of the century, and then later revived by the Louis Martini family in the Napa Valley when they planted the neighboring Monte Rosso Vineyard in the 1940s. Very respectable Cabernet Sauvignon from Glen Ellen Vineyard grapes were bottled during the 1970s by wineries such as Chateau St. Jean, Kistler and Ridge.

Mac McQuown and his fellow investors—Richard Kramlich, Ted Elliot, Dominic Paino and Andy Evans—looked upon this mountain vineyard as having great potential. They proceeded to raise the money to buy the property and then set out to make their plans to further develop it. Their original idea was to divide the property into five equal pieces, develop each individual piece and then sell the grapes. Because that idea proved more difficult to execute than expected, the group started to think that perhaps they should build a winery on the site and make their own wine.

This idea added even more difficulties and differences of opinion to the already splintering investment group. None of the group had much experience actually operating a vineyard and/or winery business—they were all avid investors. They needed help. They hired Phil Woodward and Dick Graff as consultants, at first to help them properly develop the vineyards and oversee the winery plans.

The investors had already hired architect David Sellers of Warren, Vermont, to design the unique, twin-turreted redwood winery—an efficient circular design that blended well with the surrounding natural scenery. Behind the winery, caves were dug into Mount Pisgah—removing 15,000 cubic meters of volcanic rock to provide an ideal environment for barrel aging the wines. The investor group had hired Jeff Baker as winemaker. Jeff had previously worked at Mayacamas Vineyards on the Napa Valley side of the mountains, and was very familiar with what the area had to offer. Everything seemed on track for success.

But then, as often happens, money became a problem. "They just got in way over their heads," Phil said. Two of the five partners wanted out, and they wondered if Gavilan would be interested in buying the project.

The prospect of taking over the Glen Ellen Vineyard project presented Dick and Phil with a tough decision to make. On the positive side, here was another opportunity to expand: adding another winery to the Chalone and Edna Valley operations played right into their developing multi-winery growth strategy. But the negatives were substantial. First, this was to be a winery producing Bordeaux-style wines, whereas their concept was based on producing wines based on the Burgundian varieties. Second, the partners had already incurred a substantial amount of debt—debt that would have to be assumed by Gavilan. Third, and more important, where in the world would they find the money to do the deal?

"For a lot of reasons, including that we knew these people and because there was some family involved here, we decided to go ahead and try to make a deal," Phil said. "Even though it wasn't really a perfect fit with our Burgundian plan, we thought, okay, if they can really make that good a Cabernet, then we probably ought to get into the Cabernet business."

So, Phil and Dick came up with a proposal to buy out the partners and take over the operation. Originally, the idea was to give them stock in Gavilan Vineyards, Inc. in exchange for their ownership interest in Glen Ellen Vineyard. However, two of the partners did not want stock –they wanted cash. So Phil had to figure out how to raise some more money. "It was a real tough nut financially because, in order to do the deal, we had to borrow a lot of money," Phil said. "I remember telling Wells Fargo Bank that the way we would pay the money back would be to go public. They just sat there and said, 'Sure you are.' But by this time, William Hambrecht [a respected investment banker] was on our board and I said, 'Well, Hambrecht is going to do it—Bill is on our board.' And they said 'Okay.' They believed us."

With that, Gavilan Vineyards, Inc. had a third winery under its umbrella. Was it getting a little crowded in there?

Both Dick and Phil knew that there was a tremendous amount of work to do with the Glen Ellen Vineyard project. "The original partners had gotten in way over their heads with the design of the winery, with the architect," Phil said. "The first step was to begin to bring everything back down to earth."

Phil had to make some pretty tough decisions about the project early on. "The architect had all these assistants, all these other high-priced consultants," Phil said. "So, when we took over, I fired them all except for the architect himself. There were things about the winery that we simply had to put on hold—others that we had to drop entirely. These were decisions that we had to make; we had to save the business because it wasn't going to make it. The winery took seven or eight years to complete because of that."

On the positive side, the new venture had well-established vineyards and a skilled winemaker in Jeff Baker, and Dick turned his efforts now to oversee the vineyard and winery development with an eye toward the venture's first vintage in 1981. The wine from that first vintage was produced at the Edna Valley winery.

So, despite all the negatives, Glen Ellen Vineyard was on its way to its public debut—labels had been designed and everything was ready for launch when the unthinkable happened: another wine business popped up with the name "Glen Ellen Winery."

"The Benziger family had created the Glen Ellen Winery brand and was just getting it launched in the marketplace," Phil said. "We were disappointed but we also did not want to get involved in another 'Stag's Leap' type of dispute over the name [where several wineries with similar names fought over the use rights for years] and end up with lots of legal bills and even more consumer confusion. We decided to abandon the Glen Ellen Vineyard name." But that course of action meant they would need another name, and quickly.

"We decided to make a story out of it," Phil added. "We went to several wine writers, told them the story and suggested that they ask their readers for name suggestions. I don't know how many hundreds of names we received, but most of them just didn't fit. Then the assistant winemaker on the property at the time, Rob McBryde, came up with a name—'Carmenet.' He said it was from a book by Emile Peynaud, in the introductory chapter. There's a story about how all the grapes from Bordeaux descend from the Carmenet family, both red and white. It just made sense to all of us. If this was going to be our 'Bordeaux' winery, then why not give it a name that describes the Bordeaux grape varieties we were going to specialize in? And, as I like to say now, we figured that if you could pronounce 'Cabernet' and 'Chevrolet,' you could pronounce Carmenet," Phil said.

And so Carmenet became the third winery under the Gavilan Vineyards, Inc. umbrella and released its first wines under the new label from the 1982 vintage. The first wine under the Carmenet label was a Meritage blend made predominantly of Cabernet Sauvignon. This very successful debut wine is the direct ancestor of today's Moon Mountain Estate Reserve red wine.

As Phil and Dick began to concentrate on building Carmenet, they worked with Jeff Baker not only to develop wines for the marketplace, but to refine and improve the vineyard plantings on the mountain. "There was a lot of weird stuff up there—old Zinfandel and Pinot Noir, but it was mostly Cabernet Sauvignon," Phil said, "We tore the weird stuff out and planted more Cabernet Sauvignon as well as some Merlot and Cabernet Franc."

Phil and Dick also felt that Carmenet needed a white wine to balance the product line, and so they called again on their partners at Edna Valley, the Nivens. "We went to Paragon and said, 'We want to buy your Sauvignon Blanc, but we also want some Sémillon—so plant Sémillon and we'll take it all,'" Phil said. Thus Carmenet's Sauvignon Blanc-Sémillon Paragon Vineyard Reserve was born.

As 1982 DREW TO A CLOSE UP ON THE MOUNTAIN at Carmenet—and elsewhere across the growing Gavilan Vineyards empire—small changes served to focus the company on the tasks at hand. Among those changes was the company's sometimes-stormy involvement with Mount Eden Vineyards. Management of that estate came to an end when the new owners decided to go their own way.

Even with these changes, both Phil and Dick knew that they had their work cut out for them. Gavilan Vineyards, Inc. needed to grow sales, control rising costs and raise more money to fund its continued growth plans as well as pay down its burgeoning debt.

Little did either of them know that the company's most important and most interesting period lay just around the corner.

12 | *Uncharted Seas: Gavilan Goes Public*

BY LATE 1983, Dick Graff and Phil Woodward knew their company had a problem. Put simply, they needed more money.

Not that things weren't going well—they were. Sales had been growing steadily, up to $2.3 million by the end of 1983, and the company had "made lemonade" out of the lemons of the drought years by creating the Edna Valley partnership and a custom label program and by acquiring Carmenet. The company had been profitable since 1979 but would show a net loss of $38,000 in 1983, due to the Carmenet acquisition. The trend for Gavilan Vineyards, Inc. was definitely upwards, but in a capital-intensive, relatively low-margin business like the wine business, it's nearly impossible to finance and sustain growth through excess cash flow alone. Large amounts of money, whether in the form of equity financing or debt financing are required to keep the wheels rolling and the momentum going.

By 1983, the company had incurred a substantial amount of debt doing the things it needed to do to grow. That debt had financed, among other things, the Carmenet acquisition, the new winery and caves at Carmenet, and the acquisition of the Macwood Vineyard and the Creal property for Chalone. "Looking back on the financials now, we had something like $3 million or $4 million worth of debt, and we needed to do something about it," Phil said.

Phil Woodward was no stranger to raising money. In the more than 10 years he had been involved with Gavilan, he had raised money for the company through private placements four times. Phil knew that the company couldn't continue to carry the amount of debt it had incurred for much longer. He also knew that the company needed additional funding not only to reduce its debt, but also to give it the wherewithal to continue growing.

Phil's initial idea was to put together another private round of equity funding. But a seemingly far-fetched idea from a friend and Gavilan investor would soon change that plan and the entire company forever.

WILLIAM HAMBRECHT BEGAN HIS CAREER in the securities business in 1958 and, in 1968, co-founded Hambrecht & Quist, a San Francisco-based investment banking firm specializing in emerging high-growth technology companies. He is widely acknowledged as one of the true innovators and leaders in the capital-providing business. Hambrecht has been instrumental in the early strength and success of noteworthy companies such as Apple Computer, Genentech, Adobe Systems, Odwalla, Samuel Adams and many others.

In addition to his talents and reputation as a venture capitalist, Bill Hambrecht is also a wine lover. It was in this role that he came to know of Phil Woodward, Dick Graff and Chalone some years prior to 1983.

"I met Bill Hambrecht on a tennis court in Tiburon," Phil said. "We got to know each other that way first, and I found out how much he loved wine." Soon Phil had persuaded Bill to invest in the company—as a private investor, not through Hambrecht & Quist. And soon Bill had brought other individuals from the firm to Gavilan as private investors.

When Phil told Bill Hambrecht that he needed to raise more money, Bill's response was not what he expected.

"My proposal was to go back and do another private offering," Phil said. "But Bill Hambrecht said, 'Gee, you know, why don't we try a public offering?' He felt that the company was a good candidate to go public because it had a lot of sex appeal, a lot of romance to it. Hambrecht & Quist, as a firm, had been doing a lot of deals in Europe where people knew something about wine, and Bill thought they could place some of the stock there. Bill thought it was a great story."

But wait a minute. Taking a small wine company public? That's unheard of, isn't it? Traditional public companies were usually the big, blue chip icons of industry. And in the early 1980s, the focus of many public offerings—including the offerings backed by Hambrecht & Quist—were the nascent high tech companies of the just emerging Silicon Valley.

Taking a company like Gavilan public was definitely unconventional. But it was not without precedent. Both the Taylor Wine Company of New York and Rodney Strong and Peter Friedman's Tiburon Vintners preceded Gavilan as public wine companies. But with backing from Bill Hambrecht and Hambrecht & Quist, who knows, Phil mused, it might just work.

PHIL BEGAN THE PROCESS of proposing the idea of a public offering to Gavilan's board of directors. At that time, the board comprised six individuals, Dick Graff, Phil Woodward, Conger Fawcett, Jack Chambers, John McQuown and Paul Hawken. Five of the six had been associated with Chalone pretty much from the beginning—Mac McQuown was Phil's brother-in-law and investment partner when Phil decided to join Chalone; Conger Fawcett was the company's first and, to that point, only attorney; and Jack Chambers was a friend from way back who was also distributing the company's wines through his Chambers & Chambers Inc. importing and distribution firm. The relative newcomer to the board was Paul Hawken.

"Dick met Paul Hawken through the Zen Center, and, because of that, although Dick wasn't a Buddhist by any means, he did know a lot of those people," Phil said. "Paul was on the board of the Zen Center. That's how they met. Paul had written a number of books about the new economy and small businesses. He had his own company, Smith and Hawken, which at the time produced high-quality garden tools, and that's how he and I met. So Paul became a member of our board and then, a few years later, I went on the board at Smith and Hawken."

Deciding to do the public offering was not a simple subject handled as one item of business at one board meeting. It was a complicated proposition that required a lot of discussion, especially for a company and a board that had never even considered such an action, much less taken a company public.

"It probably took around six months to really discuss and make the final decision on going public," Phil said. "There was some reluctance on the part of the board that once you're public, you've got additional costs. There was reluctance that if you're public, you've got to reveal a lot of information about the internal operations of the company that instinctively you don't want to do. And then what kind of obligations do you have to the existing shareholders, let alone the people who might want to own stock in us? Well, Bill Hambrecht was pretty persuasive. He said, 'Look, it's a lot more efficient to raise this kind of money, and we can raise more money this way. The kinds of costs you're talking about are not that much, really, and the kinds of information you have to reveal—everything is done at the market anyway, so why worry about it?' So I'd have to say that Hambrecht was really the person who felt like we could do it and everyone else pretty much fell in line. And as an entrepreneur at heart, I thought it was both exciting and a great way to create shareholder value and wealth."

So the Gavilan board decided to approve the idea of taking the company public. In doing so, the board decided that two important changes needed to be made. First, the company needed to add two additional directors to the board to give it a broader-based credibility. One of these new directors was to be Bill Hambrecht; the other was Ted Marks, a long-time acquaintance and, more importantly, an executive at Castle & Cook, a large and well-known agricultural concern.

The other important item involved the company's name. Bill Hambrecht and the board felt that Gavilan Vineyards, Inc. wasn't a viable name for the new public company. For this important new direction for the company, the decision was made to reach back to the company's roots and rename the company officially what everyone called it casually. The new company name was to be Chalone, Incorporated.

The next step: create a prospectus and take it on the road.

"It was clear that I would be the one to write the prospectus," Phil said, "along with the lawyers—both ours and the Hambrecht & Quist lawyers at the time—and that was going to take a long time, because there wasn't a prospectus out there to copy. And it did—it took hours upon hours to sit down and write that prospectus from scratch."

"I had never done anything like that," Phil continued. "It's amazing the number of hours and days you sit in a room and review and go over and argue back and forth about what you want to put in and not put in. I don't know how many months that must have taken—six anyway. But that was my job to do, and then, of course, when we were ready I would do the road show with the representative of Hambrecht & Quist."

Drafting the prospectus and planning the "road show" of meetings with potential investors and investor syndicates was only part of the process of taking Chalone public. There were also the company's internal systems—accounting, sales, business reporting—that had to be aligned with the way a public company operates. And, of course, there were the employees and the company's current investor group to consider.

"There were a number of internal matters to consider," Phil said. "From an accounting standpoint, we'd had a number of profitable years, but the Carmenet acquisition—because of the way that they were losing money and the way we had to account for that when we consolidated the companies—eventually threw us in a small loss position again. So there was a lot of discussion of whether or not we should have ever bought Carmenet in the first place—it was going to show a loss on a consolidated basis and force us to go public with numbers that weren't as good as they would have been otherwise. But we had already made that decision; we were there, and we had to get out and move on. Other than that, internally we were fine. We had everything except a controller—my sister had been serving in that function—but that wasn't going to work for a public company. I hired the accountant from our CPA firm at the time, Tom Riordan. Tom became the controller of the company as we went public."

ONCE THE PROSPECTUS WAS COMPLETED and ready for distribution, it was time to get on the road and sell the idea of a public wine company named Chalone, Incorporated to the investment community.

And while Phil Woodward had been on the road raising money and selling wine for Chalone for more than 10 years, the road show for this public offering was a totally different world for him. His partner for this all-important phase of going public was to be a Hambrecht & Quist executive by the name of Jim Sullivan.

"Jim was great. He could really tell the story," Phil said. "And we're still friends after all these years—he's still with Hambrecht & Quist. He didn't know anything about wine, but he could tell the story from a financial standpoint that I couldn't."

The story was about an almost absurdly small wine company raising money through a public offering. It was about a company committed to producing high-quality wines from distinct vineyard locations. It was about a company committed to owning its vineyards. It was about a company with solid, even visionary management. The story was about raising capital for expansion and retiring growth-producing debt. And it was a story about a small wine company with a big name on the board of directors—Bill Hambrecht.

"But the bottom line was, it was still real small," Phil said. "A lot of people would show up at these road show meetings just because they couldn't believe that somebody in our position was doing this. And they probably wouldn't have even been there if not for Bill Hambrecht and Hambrecht & Quist."

Phil and Jim Sullivan started their road show in Paris at the elegant Hôtel de Crillon. And instead of the more traditional morning presentation, they had a luncheon at the hotel and served Chalone wines. "We started in Paris because Hambrecht had been doing so many road shows in Europe in 1982 and 1983, he had a lot of credibility; they knew how to draw people," Phil said. "The place was packed. This was my first presentation, too, and, of course, I wasn't going to do it in French. I had to do it in English and I was really, really nervous. I'm sure it probably showed. I have no idea how many of those people ever bought into the offering—probably none. We went to Zurich, Geneva, Glasgow, Edinburgh and London, and, by the time we left, we had sold about 25 percent of the offering. If you look at the 'tombstone,' you'll see that four or five firms from the syndicate are based in Europe."

From Europe, the duo moved on to presentations in New York and Chicago, then on to the West Coast for meetings in Los Angeles and San Francisco.

"San Francisco was the last presentation we did and it was at the Hyatt Regency Embarcadero," Phil said. "We must have had a good 150 people there for that luncheon. We were in the middle of the presentation when there was an earthquake—a pretty good one at that—and everybody went under the tables. When it was over, I got back up and said, 'See, I'll do anything to get your attention.'"

For Phil, Dick and the rest of the Chalone team, all that was left to be done was wait and see what would happen. For Phil Woodward, the time right up to the closing of the public offering was filled with sleepless nights.

"Right up until the last minute, I thought that we could probably get

$9 per share, but you don't know until it's over," Phil said. "So, on the last day you sit in this office with the syndicate manager while they're making all the phone calls and pulling in all the chits. Then they tell you, 'This is it. We can do this; if you don't want it, then we don't go.' By that time, these guys have spent so much time and money that you're going to do what it takes to get it done."

The public offering for Chalone, Incorporated—CHLN on the NASDAQ exchange—closed at $8 per share and that per-share price worked out to $5.4 million in proceeds for the company. The total market capitalization of the company after the public offering was $18.5 million. That's not bad for a company with just $2 million in sales. And it wasn't bad considering that the four previous private placements Phil had put together for the company raised between $250,000 and $500,000 each.

ONE OF THE GOALS of the process of taking a company public is to generate a "buzz" about the company and its story. The hope is that the buzz is positive and therefore helps sell the offering and raise more money for the company.

One of the unique and interesting things about the Chalone public offering was that it provided an unprecedented peek behind the curtain—a look at the inside workings of a modern, growing wine company. This kind of opportunity was virtually unheard of in the closely knit, closely held California wine industry of the early 1980s. Information on the internal operations and financial performance of a winery was almost never available unless it was provided voluntarily by the winery. And it never was. Never before had a wine company completely laid out everything it had for all to see—friends and foes alike.

The intense curiosity about the mystique of the wine business—the dark cellars, the artisans turned businessmen, the assumption that if the wine was good the business must be successful—quickly catapulted the

Chalone, Incorporated prospectus to the top of the "must have, must read" list. It was, indeed, a very revealing, humbling and at times embarrassing experience for Phil Woodward and Dick Graff.

"We knew that all of our competitors were going to at least buy 10 shares so they could see how well we were doing, what they thought we were doing wrong, and how much better or worse off they were than us," Phil said. "Everyone would be looking for how much money the company was making, as well as how much money Dick or I were making as individuals. We knew we would be faced with all those things."

As painful as that process could be, Phil was not too worried. "We didn't have a whole lot to hide—nothing to hide, really. It's just there were some insider things we had done over the years that were perfectly normal, even commonplace in smaller, privately held businesses that all of a sudden were out in the open for everyone to see, and possibly to misunderstand," Phil said. "I took a lot of heat from people within the industry saying, 'What are you doing this for?' and we had to deal with our share of unfair criticism as well. That was tough."

Perhaps the most stinging of that criticism came just after the offering closed in an article published in the May 16, 1984, issue of *Wine Spectator*. Written by Dan Berger, then a business and wine writer for the *San Diego Union,* the article—entitled "Is Chalone a 'Breed Apart'? Winery Goes Public But Analysts Call Its Stock Offering a Financial Gamble"—was harsh in its judgment of the company's prospects for success, its motivations for going public and its value as an investment.

"That *Wine Spectator* article was really demoralizing to me," Phil said. "They sort of made a joke out of us. My wife, Diane, was really supportive of me because I was really down. I mean—we didn't get the price per share that we thought we were going to get—we'd hoped to get $10; we got $8—so we didn't quite raise as much money as we wanted-ed. And then to be slammed by that article. Very quickly, though, I realized that we had already crossed the bridge—we were committed, we were public. We had a job to do. I think the one thing that helped me most was knowing that Bill Hambrecht was on the board and there to help. I knew that we were going to make it."

While the critics sounded off against the company and the wisdom of going public, Phil took considerable solace in the realization that what they had accomplished was far more than simply to raise money. He knew that he could have raised the money without going public. "Raising the kind of money we needed through additional private placements would have taken a lot more time and we would have had to find maybe 10 people of substantial means to get it, but they would have owned a good part of the company by that time," Phil said. "That would have changed the whole dynamic of the company, and that was something we didn't want. We wanted money but we didn't want any big person or persons to come in, own a big chunk and change the way we were building the company."

Phil and Dick absolutely believed that they had a strong vision, the strategic plan to deliver the vision, a board of directors that supported and believed in the vision and the talented team to execute the plan. Going public not only gave the company access to the capital it needed, it gave the company's biggest fans—wine consumers—the chance to literally buy in to the vision.

"We felt that if we could get public shareholders, then these shareholders would become not only our customers, but more importantly our ambassadors," Phil said. "Even before we went public, it was clear to us that the role of shareholders as ambassadors was one that really fit our company. Before the public offering we had 300 shareholders and it was easy to see that there was a lot of enthusiasm there. But there really wasn't any alternative for our customers and others who really wanted to buy into the company—to 'own a piece of the rock,' so to speak—or a piece of the vineyard. Taking the company public allowed the average wine consumer to be an owner, and to spread the word to all of his or her friends. We figured we could probably do well with that kind of a story."

Filled with cautious optimism, Phil Woodward, Dick Graff and Chalone, Incorporated turned to face the challenges ahead. Bolstered by the proceeds of the public offering and the support of hundreds of shareholder/ambassadors, they felt good about the prospects for the future.

13 | *Back to Business*

As PHIL WOODWARD SAT AT HIS DESK in the summer of 1984, the frenetic and rapid-fire pace of the public offering behind him, it didn't take long for him to settle back into business as usual.

Business as usual meant the aftermath of the Carmenet acquisition. The emergence of Carmenet as a growing brand in the Chalone portfolio meant that there had to be a slight realignment of the company's vision of itself.

"With the Carmenet acquisition, we committed ourselves to another strategy to some degree," Phil said. "We weren't just going to be the Burgundians of California. By acquiring Carmenet, we in essence said 'Okay, what we're really going to do is have multiple wineries representing the top varietals.' Carmenet was going to be our Bordeaux winery. Terroir, place and the right varietals in the right place became the real vision."

While the public offering solved many of the company's immediate problems—the most important being the reduction of the company's debt, it didn't change the focus or the immediate action plan for Phil or Dick.

"The immediate focus was Carmenet; getting it profitable and getting the winery finished," Phil said. "The fact is, we stepped up and took it over, and now it was up to us to make it work."

The challenge, according to Phil, first of all was to make Carmenet profitable the old-fashioned way: by selling enough wine. "We had Chambers & Chambers on the street for us in California, and they were doing just fine. Our out-of-state distributor sales were handled in house by Barbara Barnhart. At that time it was an allocation game; you had to make sure you satisfied everybody with his or her allocation, " Phil said.

The "buzz" generated around the new public company also went a long way to help boost the company's wine sales in 1984, including sales of Carmenet wines.

Meanwhile, more than 200 miles to the south, back on the Gavilan benchland, Phil and Dick were faced with a problem. They needed space for more wine storage at Chalone. At the same time, vintners all over California were rediscovering the value of caves for storing their wines. Digging into their hillsides, winemakers found out what their 19th-century counterparts knew well: caves were a great way to keep wine under perfect conditions—cool, dark and humid—without air conditioning, at relatively little expense and with low maintenance.

The first contemporary California vintners to understand this were Jack and Jamie Davies of Schramsberg in the Napa Valley. When they bought Schramsberg in 1965, 103 years after Jacob Schram established it, they found caves that Chinese laborers had hacked out of the hillsides with picks, shovels and brute strength. When Schramsberg needed more space to store sparkling wine during its secondary fermentation, Jack Davies called Alf Burtleson. A civil engineer, Burtleson had been a tunnel contractor for 21 years. Working with his roadheader, a rock-mining machine whose front is shaped like a long snout and has a large rotating ball with knifelike ridges, Burtleson dug out an additional 1,200 linear feet of caves for Schramsberg.

"Jack Davies gave us the idea, and Alf Burtleson gave us the caves," Dick said after Burtleson burrowed 100 feet into the hills east of the winery. Next, he dug out a second tunnel that extended like an arm from the first and then angled out to form another entrance. In all, the tunnels gave Chalone an additional 3,500 square feet of wine storage space. Completed in 1984, they cost about $50 per square foot, "about half of what it would cost to build an above-ground wine aging warehouse," Dick said.

The Gavilan benchland had its own opinion of the value of Chalone's new caves. What was unknown—and unknowable—before digging began was that the caves would run directly above underground thermal activity that kept the temperature higher than the cool temperature many other wine caves enjoy. A chiller was installed, proving once again that the universal motto at Chalone is to be prepared ... and then adapt.

As an appropriate testament to the value of being adaptable, Chalone, Incorporated finished 1984, its first year as a public company, with $3.2 million in sales and $116,000 in net income—all in all a much improved picture.

THE YEAR 1985 BEGAN with the gnawing realization that, even with the public offering, the company had not raised enough money to move forward as aggressively as it wanted. That need was met through a second offering for $3 million in convertible debentures, completed in February 1985.

"Even though the pubic offering of $5.4 million was great, we still needed to get some more money," Phil said. "So, instead of going to the bank, I went to a handful of the top shareholders—after the public offering—and sold them a convertible debenture offer for $3 million. I think there were 10 people in that deal, and it was sort of a semi-private deal where they lent us the money and it was convertible into shares of company stock. Even though this was technically taking on more debt, it allowed us to pay off some of the bank debt that we had incurred without having to use all the public money to do it."

So it appeared that 1985 was going to be a busy year and a year of many "firsts" for the company. Electricity and telephone service would come to the Chalone winery on the benchland for the first time that year. The company would experiment with expanding its wine sales portfolio to include wines imported by Kermit Lynch, the Berkeley, California-based fine wine importer.

1985 was also the year that William Hamilton would join the company as Chief Financial Officer, replacing Tom Riordan, who resigned to join the Peace Corps. And Chalone, Incorporated had nearly doubled in shareholders, to 600 from the pre-public offering levels of approximately 300 shareholders.

Early in 1985 the company embarked on an experiment to expand its sales and distribution reach by offering wines for sale other than those it was producing at its three wineries.

"I felt that our strategy was to be in the high end of the wine business and that some of the wines could be imported wines, as well as our own," Phil said. "Kermit Lynch was a well-established importer of mostly high-end French wines from major as well as lesser-known wine regions. I knew him. Both Dick and I shared his vision of high quality and the importance of terroir."

Phil also felt that Chalone had a good distribution system throughout the country, as well as accounts that would be interested in carrying Kermit's wines. "Kermit, at the time, was selling everything out of his store and didn't have anybody other than himself to sell outside his local market," Phil said. "So I proposed to Kermit that he let us do all the out-of-state and Southern California distribution, and he would continue to do the retail and Northern California markets. He agreed, and so Kermit and I went off to France for weeks and went around presenting to these little guys that he had relationships with—with the idea that we could, one, buy more wine because of the increased distribution and, two, try to get exclusive distribution arrangements, which Kermit felt he could do."

The arrangement would last five years and produce respectable results. Unfortunately, low margins and the lack of exclusive distribution contracts ultimately ended the arrangement.

"He trusted me and he trusted Chalone, and that's why he agreed to do this," Phil said. "Kermit has these really loyal suppliers, but he couldn't get the exclusive contracts. That really surprised him. Some of his most ardent supporters would not give him exclusives. So all of those things finally brought it to an end. We scaled down and just did it from Southern California for a while, and even that didn't work. But it did show Kermit that he really needed to have national distribution. So the experiment was a lot of fun and we didn't lose any money; but we sure learned a hell of a lot."

As THE COMPANY CONTINUED TO EXPAND Chalone on the benchland, the lack of electricity and regular water supply became problematic. In 1985 Phil and Dick asked Pacific Gas & Electric Company how much it would cost to run a power line up to Chalone. The estimate: more than $1 million. Dick and Phil decided they could probably do it on their own for a lot cheaper. The company hired a crew of former PG&E linemen, and bought a line truck, equipment and materials. The crew completed the job in three months for $250,000. To this day, Chalone still owns –and relies on—that power line.

Electricity and a telephone on the benchland were revolutionary improvements for Chalone. Even so, the kerosene lamps were not put away; they remained a fixture in most rooms. The generators also stayed in place next to the winery under a stucco-covered structure, for emergency backup.

But there was almost nothing more precious on the benchland than water, and electricity meant, among other things, that a water line could at last be put in. Installing a water line, however, proved to be far more complicated and time-consuming than installing the power line. From the time Phil and Dick started the project in 1985 until it was completed, a year passed.

To begin, Dick searched for a parcel of land on the valley floor that had water beneath it. Before buying the parcel, he hired Ray Machsmeyer to check if there was indeed water and, if so, to pinpoint where the well should be dug. With 500 wells to his credit, Machsmeyer was the premier dowser in Monterey County. Dowsing, in fact, seems to run in the Machsmeyer family. Ray's father dowsed for himself and his friends. Ray and his twin brother dowse professionally. "My brother dowses with a forked limb but he can't tell you how deep the water is," Ray said. "I can. If I use a forked limb, it breaks in my hand; I have that much power."

For the first 35 years of his working life, Ray was a truck driver. When he realized he had dowsing ability, he switched careers. "I can feel a stream a quarter-mile away. I swing a blue crystal ball, and it has immediate response. I swing it so I can feel water in any direction. I tried whalebone, wood, regular crystal. They all work for me but not as fast as my blue crystal ball."

Ray Machsmeyer swung his blue crystal ball around the five-acre parcel Dick had found, and he proclaimed there was water beneath it. Dick bought the property, hired a well digger and had a well put in. And yes, water gushed out. But it gushed out black and smelling of hydrogen sulfide. It was useless. Ray the dowser can find water, and he can tell how deep it is; but he cannot tell if it is going to be good, clean, usable water.

Phil and Dick sold that property for the price they paid for it, but they had to pay a hefty fee for having a well put in. Undaunted, Dick looked for another parcel of land.

This time instead of having to locate and buy another property, Dick was able to get an easement allowing him to use someone else's land for a particular purpose. The property he found was down near the valley floor at the former Paul Masson vineyards that Agustin Huneeus had recently purchased.

"Agustin was a real gentleman, and we were able to negotiate for a strip of the property," Dick said. "Then I called Ray Machsmeyer again. This piece of land is on the other side of the road, closer to the river, and water does tend to get better there. Ray dowsed and proclaimed there was water. So we arranged for a new well to be sunk."

Earlier, when he was having the first well drilled, Dick began the complex process of putting in the pipeline. The first and most time-consuming step was to get easements over the many properties the pipeline would have to cross to reach up from the valley to Chalone. When he finally completed that step, he hired a company to design the pipeline. "The line would run seven miles and would have to raise the water about 1,500 feet up the mountain. We wanted 500 gallons a minute. To do that required four 50-horsepower boosters along the way."

Once the design was approved, the company began to lay the pipeline. Working with a road grader, the men dug a ditch about two feet deep, laid the eight-inch pipe and covered it. The entire seven miles of pipeline were laid in two weeks. There were minor details to be completed, but the line itself was in and ready for the well to fill it with water.

While the first well had been a failure, the second one, dug on the Huneeus property, gushed good, clean, fresh water. The pipeline, which had been built up to the first well site, was conducted over to the second well and attached. Thus, in 1986, "for the first time ever, we had water-on-demand up at Chalone," Dick said with a broad grin.

14 | *Coming to the Napa Valley*

TOWARD THE END OF 1985 a rumor started to make its way through the grapevine of winery executives and investors. It found its way to Richard Kramlich, one of the original investors in Carmenet and a friend of Phil Woodward.

The rumor was that Acacia Winery, the high-profile producer of Chardonnay and Pinot Noir in the Carneros region of southern Napa and Sonoma counties, might be up for sale.

"Dick Kramlich called me and said that he had heard Acacia was for sale, and wouldn't it make a great addition to the portfolio," Phil said. "So I called around a bit and got in touch with Paul Perret, who was an attorney and one of the partners representing the ownership group. He confirmed that the company was for sale."

The prospect of acquiring Acacia was exciting. "Acacia came out in 1979 with their first wines," Phil said. "They were real pioneers in the Carneros. Carneros Creek and Mont St. John were probably the only other wineries there before they were. Acacia was making a big splash with their vineyard-designated wines. The wines were very, very drinkable and getting a lot of press. Jerry Goldstein and Mike Richmond (Acacia's founders) were out front doing something different, and everyone—especially in California and Southern California—was really jumping on their bandwagon."

Phil began to meet with Paul Perret on a regular basis to explore the terms for a possible deal. At the time, Phil thought that they were really making progress. Then one day, the meetings just stopped. Perret explained that they had been talking to other possible buyers and that their offers were more appealing. For several months there was no communication between Phil and Perret. Phil had pretty much resigned himself to the apparent reality that the deal was gone when, out of the blue, Perret called and said that he wanted to talk again.

"This time, it really got serious—to the point where we each had our attorneys meeting on some really detailed stuff," Phil said. "It went on and on and on—that's when I began to realize that something was wrong. There were definitely some things at Acacia that the partners did not want to reveal, rumors of all kinds of things, including misappropriation of company funds. One of the more public things was that Jerry Goldstein had tried to use the Acacia name to start another winery with another partner to make Merlot and Cabernet Sauvignon. The problem was that he never let the original partners know he was using the Acacia name. And so, for a couple of years, you saw Acacia Merlot and Cabernet out on the market. The original partners decided it was time to get out, and Perret was the guy to do the deal.

Phil was trying to get to the point where he could determine whether it made any sense to make an offer on Acacia. But in order to get there, he needed information. "During the due diligence period I couldn't talk to any of the employees. I had to sign an agreement that said I wouldn't talk to them. All of the employees had to sign agreements that they wouldn't talk to me. In addition, all of the employees had to sign agreements saying they wouldn't leave. I found all of this out after the fact," Phil said.

But Phil kept plugging along, because in those days an acquisition like Acacia didn't come along every day.

"We really felt that this was a good deal for us to get into the Napa Valley," Phil said. "So I just kept hanging in there and with the help of

Bill Hambrecht, especially, we resolved the issues one by one. One of the big issues involved the Acacia partners—some partners wanted to take stock, some wanted to take cash and others wanted to take both. In the end, the deal that we struck gave the partners some cash and gave them all some stock in Chalone going forward. For the partners who didn't want to keep the stock, Bill Hambrecht agreed to resell the shares at $5.50. That way they could get liquid and we could still make the deal."

Thus, in July 1986, after nearly a year of negotiations, Chalone, Incorporated acquired Acacia Winery for $5.2 million in cash, approximately $3 million in stock and an assumption of approximately $300,000 in debt. The purchase included the Acacia winery and brand, the land that the winery was on and part ownership of the adjacent Marina Vineyard. However, the deal was not without its last-minute complications.

"Paul Perret, at the very last moment, said he wanted to be on the Chalone board," Phil said. "And that almost became a deal breaker. We eventually brought him on the board and then didn't nominate him to continue at the next annual shareholders meeting. There were other things about wine privileges. There apparently was a stash of imported wines that had been purchased using partnership money—a lot of Burgundies—and they wanted all those wines, too. Some of these little things at the last moment when you're dealing with 20 or so partners in a negotiation can get really, really annoying."

Despite the complications, Chalone ended up with an outstanding brand and a great winery facility, as well as some top-notch people who would grow with the company for years to come.

"Mike Richmond, Acacia's co-founder and evangelist, stayed with us and took over for me as Chalone's National Sales Manager. Larry Brooks stayed on as winemaker," Phil said. "I asked Sandy Garber, who had been Acacia's Southern California representative, to stay on and sell all of our wines direct to wine shops and restaurants."

The Acacia deal, while a terrific boon to the newly public Chalone, also took its toll personally on Phil Woodward. During the better part of a year that the on and off negotiations for Acacia were taking place, Phil was also dealing with troubles in his family's business in Illinois.

"At the same time I was doing all the Acacia dealings, the silica sand and mining company back in Illinois that my father and grandfather and everybody in my family had worked for was slowly dying. I chose never to work for the company, but by this time I was on the board—my father was deceased and everybody else was gone except for uncles and cousins. I was leading the charge to sell it and trying to get enough people on the company's board of directors to agree to do it. It wasn't much of a company, but it was either sell it or lose it. So I was trying to negotiate Acacia and at the same time going back to Illinois and dealing with the family stress. Both deals closed at about the same time. Two months later, I was in the hospital here with bleeding ulcers. It was a tough year, that's for sure," Phil said.

At the end of the day, however, Chalone had benefited tremendously from Phil's hard-won successes. "It was a huge step for us," Phil said. "Acacia had been a profitable company and when we bought it—even though some people said we overpaid a little bit—we ended up paying for the acquisition in five years from the profits we made. We established a foothold in Napa, bolstered our reputation for being the premier producer of Burgundy-style wines in California, and brought some really good people into the company."

The Acacia acquisition came along at a time when the company was still dealing with the aftermath of going public—paying down debt and trying to stay focused on the business at hand. They were clearly not in an acquisition mode—but an opportunity is something Phil has learned not to ignore. "We really wanted to be in the Napa Valley, and here was a good opportunity for us to do so. We took advantage of that," he said.

15 | *The Umbrella Gets Crowded*

PHIL WOODWARD REMEMBERS GETTING A CALL one day in 1987 from Michael Michaud, then the winemaker at Chalone, that "a Rothschild" had dropped by the winery to visit. Mike couldn't remember which Rothschild it was, only that he had come with Richard Peterson of The Monterey Vineyard to "see what was going on." Phil shrugged and didn't think much more about it.

Then Bill Hambrecht called and said that he'd had a conversation with Baron Eric de Rothschild about Chalone—Baron Eric had called him! Hambrecht and Baron Eric didn't know each other personally at the time, but they knew of each other. Again, Phil noted this interesting fact, but there was really not much to be done at that point.

In early 1988, the receptionist at Chalone's San Francisco office buzzed Phil and said, "There's a Mr. Rothschild on the phone for you."

"My first reaction," Phil said, "was 'Yeah, right.' It was probably another one of my college buddies calling to make jokes and get some free wine. So, playing along, I said, 'Ask him what his first name is.' "

She buzzed back. "He says his first name is Baron Eric."

"I'll take the call," Phil said.

"Sure enough, that's who it was," Phil said. "He was very cordial on the phone. He had visited Chalone before and had spoken to Bill

Hambrecht; he knew quite a bit about our company by reading the annual reports, and he was very impressed with our philosophy, in that we felt strongly about owning our own vineyards—not just buying grapes and making wine, but owning the vineyards and the land. He went on to say that their philosophy was very similar, and if I was ever in Paris, would I drop by and see him, and perhaps we could talk about doing business together."

Baron Eric de Rothschild is managing director of Les Domaines Barons de Rothschild (Lafite), the wine segment of his family's vast business and financial holdings. Les Domaines Barons de Rothschild (DBR) at the time managed the first-growth Château Lafite-Rothschild for the Rothschild family and owned Château Duhart-Milon, a classified fourth-growth estate in the Bordeaux appellation of Pauillac; Château Rieussec, producer of some of the finest Sauternes in France; Château La Cardonne, an unclassified estate in the northern Médoc and Viña los Vascos, a prestigious wine estate in Chile.

Phil wasn't in the habit of "dropping by" Paris, but he was in charge of international sales for the company, and that job did take him periodically to Switzerland. So on his next trip to Geneva, he made arrangements to meet with Baron Eric.

"I flew from Geneva to Paris and the idea was that I was going to meet him in the afternoon. His driver would pick me up at the airport and take me back. I had a same-day round-trip ticket from Geneva to Paris, because I felt that the meeting would probably last about 20 minutes if it didn't go well, and, at the outside a couple of hours if it did go well. It lasted much more than a couple of hours. It turned out we had a lot of similarities and thoughts about business and especially the wine business. It was amazing, because they're really Bordeaux people and we have always thought of ourselves as Burgundians who didn't know much about Bordeaux. But that aside, we found we had a lot in common in terms of building a wine and vineyard business," Phil said.

Phil recalled his impressions of Baron Eric at that first meeting. "First of all, I realized that he's almost exactly the same age I am, and that he speaks fluent English. He almost has a British accent, which really threw me because I thought that he would sound more like a Frenchman. Also, he obviously knew a great deal about the wine business. You might be tempted to assume that maybe he didn't know a lot about the wine business, that he just knew a lot about banking. In fact, he knew quite a bit about wine and the wine business—how the investments should be made, what the return on the investment should be and what the long-term strategy should be. I felt—and I think he did, too, that the chemistry was good enough that it made sense to try to go forward and do something together. We had talked about how that might happen; we had played around with a lot of different scenarios. And of course, it was very flattering, to me personally and the whole company, that the person who ran Château Lafite-Rothschild would be interested in doing business with us."

The meeting with Baron Eric went so well and lasted so much longer than Phil anticipated that by the time he was ready to leave, Phil realized not only that he was going to miss his flight back to Geneva, but that Baron Eric's driver had gone home for the day and he had no French currency to pay for a taxi to the airport. Baron Eric reached into his pocket, pulled out a roll of bills and said, "This ought to help you." Phil knew that once he got to the airport he could use his credit card to stay at a hotel, which he did. "I figured that if he was willing to loan me cab fare, we probably started off on a pretty good footing," Phil said.

On his way to the airport and a hotel for the night, Phil reflected on how the meeting had gone. It had gone more than well, ending in an agreement to carry on the discussions and figure out some way that the two companies could work together. And he thought about some of the possible scenarios that he and Baron Eric had discussed.

"At the time that I went to meet with Baron Eric, the company was in the process of talking with Bill Hambrecht and Hambrecht & Quist about raising some additional money, possibly another convertible debenture offering, to fund ongoing expansion at the wineries," Phil said.

When it became clear that Baron Eric was interested in investing in

Chalone, Phil asked him if he could help Chalone raise money. Baron Eric replied that he could and he would. For Phil, this became a very big incentive to try to build some kind of alliance. "He was used to raising money," Phil said. "He said he would raise it in Europe, and he could raise it cheaper and faster than Hambrecht & Quist could. So I took the discussion a little bit further by telling him how much we wanted to raise, which was around $10 million. He said that the Rothschild Bank could do it for a lesser fee, and if we were going to do a convertible debenture, he said the 5 percent rate would be good enough in Europe. Well, over here you couldn't do a convertible debenture at that time for anything less than 9 or 10 percent. So that was a huge savings if we could work together to do that."

As part of their discussions that day, Phil and Baron Eric talked about the form and structure of a relationship between their two companies. It was clear that Baron Eric wanted to make a significant investment in Chalone. Phil was open to that, but he also wanted to make some form of investment in DBR.

"It was pretty clear from the outset that Château Lafite itself was not going to be part of any deal that we would make," Phil said. "Lafite is held by the Rothschild family and managed by DBR. But DBR owned lots of other things, and Baron Eric said that we could invest in DBR. So we talked about different ways of us investing in them, and them investing in us, and raising new money. And that's about where we left it."

The next morning, Phil flew back to Geneva with all kinds of possibilities darting in and out of his mind. It was a truly unexpected turn of events for him and for Chalone.

Once Phil returned to San Francisco, arrangements were made to have representatives from DBR 's New York office come to California to start exploring the specifics of a possible deal. It was during these discussions that Phil and the management team at Chalone first met Christophe Salin, the president of DBR and the man responsible for the day-to-day management of all DBR activities.

Meanwhile, Phil still had a lot of work to do to convince his board of directors that making a deal with DBR was even a good idea, much less something they should pursue immediately.

Phil sat down with Bill Hambrecht, who gave Phil some very valuable advice as he had so many times in the past. "Always remember that the Rothschilds are bankers as well as wine people, and that they'll always be looking at it from that standpoint. On the other hand, to be able to have them as partners is a once-in-a-lifetime opportunity, and if you don't take that opportunity, someone else will."

"We had some real disagreements among our board at the time on whether or not we should do this," Phil said. "Some felt very strongly that this was just not the way we should go. Their position was that we had our own strategy; we should stay here and just keep on doing what we're doing. We had Hambrecht & Quist to help us raise money and we were making money, so why do this? But the majority of us, including Dick and I, felt that this was an opportunity to grow the company in a direction with the help of a prestigious company with prestigious brands. DBR kept telling us that they were investors not operators. Not silent investors, mind you, but we would still run the company."

What really crystallized the decision for Dick, Phil and the board was a comment one of the board members made. He said, "The Rothschilds always buy, they never sell. If you're looking for a long-term partner who really cares about the wine industry, I think you have the right one."

The decision to move ahead with DBR and the Rothschilds had the unfortunate effect of hastening the exit of Bill Hambrecht from Chalone. "I think when we made that decision, Hambrecht decided he did not want to stay," Phil said. "But it wasn't just for that reason. At the time, he was getting infatuated with the wine side of the wine business. He already had a lot of vineyards, and I remember discussing with him that he was either going to have to be a vineyard person and sell to lots of wineries, or go to the wine side and take on a lot more headaches. Well, he chose to go with all the headaches. By starting his own winery, Belvedere, he decided that he couldn't stay with us. Shortly thereafter, he sold his shares in Chalone to Rothschild."

From that point, the negotiations between Chalone and DBR picked up speed, but it was not a simple or speedy process.

"I like to say that, despite the lawyers and accountants, we came to an agreement," Phil said. "It was a very complicated deal, and as I look back on it, it probably shouldn't have happened the way it did. Baron Eric did not want to invest in our company through common stock. That made it more difficult, because if he invested in equity in our company, that would have been relatively straightforward. Also, we decided to walk before we ran, so the initial deal signed in February 1989 was essentially a 6 percent ownership in each other. Their stake in us was represented by just over $3 million in convertible debentures in us, and ours was represented by just over $3 million in "ordinary shares" in DBR. Two years later, the cross-ownership increased to 20 percent of each other's business."

As soon as the deal was announced, the press—both mainstream and wine—were all over the story, each with their own unique take on the deal:

"U.S.-French Wineries in Stock-Swap Accord" —*New York Times*
"Chalone, Rothschild Plan to Invest in Each Other"

—*Los Angeles Times*
"Chalone to Join Rothschild Team"   —*San Francisco Examiner*
"S.F. Winemaker, Lafite Rothschild in Deal"

—*San Francisco Chronicle*
"Chalone, Rothschild Join Forces: Agreement Reached
 for Equity Swap"   —*Wine Spectator*
"Wine Giants Join Hands"   —*Marin Independent Journal*
"Stock Swap Lets French Vintner Expand Business"

—*San Francisco Business Times*

"Once the deal was done, we got a lot of press in San Francisco and beyond. I couldn't believe some of the pictures and stories that were written about us. Some of it was probably due to the Mondavi-Rothschild alliance in Opus One. Even though it was a different Rothschild—the English side of the Rothschilds being the ones involved in Opus through their ownership of Château Mouton-Rothschild—it really was a pretty unusual thing to have two Rothschild ventures in

California," Phil said.

Another side effect of the deal announcement was a dramatic rise in the price of Chalone stock. In the three days following the announcement of the Chalone-DBR deal, the price of one share of Chalone stock jumped from $11 to as high as $15.

And when Baron Eric said he could help Chalone raise money in Europe, he wasn't kidding. "One day, Eric called and said that some of his friends were going to come up with the money that he said he could raise for us," Phil said. "He said that he was going to have them all for dinner at the château and would I come over for dinner? Coming over for dinner meant I flew from San Francisco to London and from London to Bordeaux, was picked up by a driver who took me to the château, getting me there essentially in time for dinner. Shortly after my arrival, all these cars roll up and all these guys get out—all dressed in black with bodyguards all over the place. There were no women at all. We have this great dinner. Eric was introducing everybody in about three or four languages. I was there because I was 'Mr. Chalone.' If these men were going to put up this money, they wanted to make sure there really was a person. I didn't have to say anything; I didn't have to show anything; I just had to be there. But we drank some of the most fabulous wines you could ever imagine. After cigars and Lafite Cognac, they all got back in their cars and left. I got up the next morning and caught a flight back to San Francisco—deal done. They wired the money the next day into the Rothschild Bank in Paris and then it was wired it to us."

This got Phil thinking that, in all the years he had been raising money, perhaps he'd been doing it the hard way. "I couldn't believe it! I mean— no SEC [Securities and Exchange Commission] registration, no nothing. No prospectus. Nothing. He just talked to them, said 'Here's the finances; here's the deal; this is what we're going to do.' The response: 'Eric's behind it. Where do I send the money?' This money, combined with the funds I raised in Switzerland through our distributor there and through a banking contact that Bill Hambrecht provided, resulted in $8.5 million in financing," Phil said.

∾

SHORTLY AFTER THE CHALONE-DBR DEAL WAS FINALIZED and while the company was adjusting to the new cross-ownership arrangement, a new player came to the table and did so at first in a mysterious and alarming way.

Richard Hojel was a sophisticated investor, wine lover and the patriarch of his family's business and investment interests. Richard and his family were prominent in Mexico City's business community with some investments in the United States. In addition, he and two or three other Mexican businessmen had started a winery in Baja California's Guadalupe Valley, outside of Ensenada, called Monte Xanic. It was and still is the premier quality wine producer in all of Mexico.

Hojel found out about Chalone through a business friend who handled a lot of his investments. He decided to buy some shares in the company, because he liked what Chalone was doing with its direct sales efforts through the catalog and thought that he would like to emulate that at Monte Xanic. The more he read about Chalone, the more he liked the company and the more shares he bought.

At that same time one of Chalone's directors, Richard Kramlich, and his wife had been a guest of Richard Hojel at his home in Mexico City. Both the Hojels and the Kramlichs had interests in modern art, thus the occasion of the dinner. To the Kramlichs' surprise, Richard Hojel served not only his Monte Xanic wines, but also wines from Chalone Vineyard. Hojel told Kramlich that he was a big fan of Chalone and that he was a shareholder. Upon the Kramlichs' return to San Francisco, Dick Kramlich told Phil the story.

"I didn't pay much attention to it until one Sunday I was at my home at Chalone and I got a call from Dick Kramlich," Phil said. "Dick said that he had just received a call from Richard Hojel, who said that on Monday he was going to tell the SEC he now owned more than 5 percent of our stock, as required by SEC regulations. Dick thought I should call Richard and find out a little bit more about him. So I did. I called him the next week and we made arrangements for him to come to San Francisco. We put together a dinner at Dick Kramlich's home. Richard said that he would bring one of his sons with him. We notified the Rothschilds about this. They had no idea who he was, but they had their banking people in Mexico City on it fast. When I said he was coming for dinner in San Francisco the following week, they said they'd send Christophe Salin over to meet him, too."

The Kramlichs hosted a dinner for Richard. Then there was a second special dinner so that Christophe Salin could meet him as well. At both dinners there was a lot of "who are you?" and "why did you do this?" talk.

It turned out that Richard was an exceedingly charming man. He had lost both his arms when he had been electrocuted in a freak accident. But he had a strong desire for quality wine, and he wanted to make Monte Xanic the best winery in Mexico. He explained again and again that he hadn't intended to exceed the 5 percent mark with his investment in Chalone.

"As time went on after that, he and his family became even bigger investors in Chalone," Phil said. "Richard became a key person for us at the board level. Everybody had an awful lot of respect for him, and because he knew a lot about American business. He became the chairman of our executive committee because he could relate to both the French and the American way of doing business. He became in many ways a facilitator and conciliator, he helped things move along better. Richard Hojel died in 1995, and we miss him. He was a great man."

The Hojel family continued to stay involved in Chalone and currently owns 15 percent of the company, making it the second largest single shareholder of the company.

Today, Monte Xanic is run by one of Richard Hojel's sons, Mark Hojel. "Mark is also on the Chalone board now," Phil said. "He's a good influence and brings a different perspective to the board. The Hojels are a wonderful family, and their relationship with the Rothschilds has always been good. We're happy to have them as part of the team."

TEN YEARS BEFORE, in the early 1980s, Phil Woodward found himself in Seattle at a luncheon along with Dan Duckhorn of Duckhorn Vineyards in the Napa Valley. The luncheon was in conjunction with their mutual distributor in Seattle and was being held at Rosselini's Other Place—a restaurant that at the time was known for its extensive wine list.

After the luncheon, the owner of the restaurant generously insisted that they choose something off the wine list to try. One of Phil's passions over the years has been to taste and collect wines from every wine-producing state in the United States, as well as every wine-producing country. He had not yet had the opportunity to taste a Washington wine, so he enthusiastically dived into the restaurant's extensive selection.

Phil pored over the list until one particular wine caught his eye. "I saw this Chardonnay on the list called Woodward Canyon, and I thought, 'Hey, why not? It's a great name, maybe it's a great wine,'" he said. "When they brought it out, I liked the packaging and I was also incredibly impressed with the wine. I thought to myself, Wow! This is Chalone all over again! It was serious stuff." Phil asked about the wine and the producer, and the restaurateur told him that it was a guy named Rick Small, located out in Walla Walla, and that it was his second vintage.

Phil decided right then and there that he had to find out more. Instead of going back to California, he took his rented car and drove the nearly 200 miles southeast through the Cascade Mountains to Lowden, Washington, a tiny town just before the much larger Walla Walla. "If you blink, you'll miss this town," Phil said. "I could barely find the little sign for Woodward Canyon Winery, but I did and pulled in and asked for Rick Small. He was there. He was also the only employee."

Phil introduced himself and was surprised when Small replied, "I know Chalone. I've been there and I try to model the way I make wines after the way you guys do."

"When he visited Chalone, he met Peter Graff, who at the time was the winemaker. Rick learned a lot from that visit, and I was amazed to see that he was doing everything exactly the same as we did at Chalone, down to using the same barrels," Phil said. "We hit it off immediately. I don't know if it was that day, but shortly thereafter I asked him if we could sell his wines outside of the Northwest. He was only selling his wines in Washington, Oregon and Idaho at the time. So we struck up a deal for Chalone to sell his wines outside of those three states. That wasn't a hell of a lot of wine, obviously, but it was a step forward, and then we also put him in our catalog."

Small was also making some red wine as well, especially Cabernet Sauvignon. Phil was quickly convinced that Washington state Cabernet, and especially those from Woodward Canyon, had tremendous potential. His colleagues at Chalone were skeptical. They humored him at first, and nobody took him or the wines too seriously. But when Phil wanted to make a commitment to start selling these Cabernets, his staff started to object, saying, "You just can't make great red wines up there."

Phil needed an undisputable way to make his point. "We'd have these tastings around the table in our San Francisco offices, so I started putting the wines in brown bags. Whenever we were doing Cabernets, I'd include not only the wines we made at Carmenet and a selection of other California Cabernets, but I'd also stick in a bottle of Woodward Canyon. Every time I did that, Woodward Canyon would come out either in first or second place. Mike Richmond was the first one to say, 'This is incredible. They can do this up there? Who would have thought?' Both Dick and Jeff Baker kept trying to resist the fact that the wine was any good. We kept rating it first or second every time. And the wine started to sell, especially after the *Wine Spectator* put it in their Top 100 listing one year."

Washington wines were all of a sudden starting to get noticed. Phil saw an opportunity to grow the company into an area that was just emerging on the U.S. wine scene. "I asked Rick Small if he would be willing to sell all or part of Woodward Canyon to us. Rick wasn't interested. He'd say 'Well, maybe someday, but not now.' I told him that we wanted to be in Washington and that if we couldn't be a part of Woodward Canyon, then we would like to do something with him. I told him, 'Think about it. Is there something we can do together?'"

BY THIS TIME, the Chalone board of directors was getting excited about some kind of venture in Washington state. So when Rick Small told Phil that he had some friends in Walla Walla who had started a vineyard at a place called Canoe Ridge who might be interested in a partner to help them expand, he was both excited and a little cautious.

"To start with, I had never heard of Canoe Ridge, but, hey, I hadn't heard of Washington much, either," Phil said. "We put together a meeting in Portland with some of the key people, including Rick, and we sat in a room talking about how we might do a deal. What they were looking for was some recognition and somebody who had some money."

The parties agreed that day that Chalone would become a 50-percent partner in the Canoe Ridge Vineyard venture and that the grapes from the vineyard would be sold to Chalone. Then Chalone would build a winery on the property and own it.

Phil's first visit to the Canoe Ridge Vineyard was an eye opener. For him, it brought back a very distinct memory.

"Going to Canoe Ridge, like a lot of eastern Washington, was just like seeing Chalone for the first time," Phil said. "You wonder how anything could grow out there until you see the rivers. The Columbia River is like a moving ocean, and you don't see it because everything out there is so flat. All of a sudden you come right up on it and wow—there it is!

"Walla Walla, on the other hand, is an old, old town of about 50,000 people. It's been about 50,000 people for about 50 years, and there's a lot of heritage there. Whitman College is there. Walla Walla is right at the foot of the Blue Mountains. It's a beautiful town, it rains a lot more there than it does in the other parts of eastern Washington, and it's always been agriculturally oriented. But what I found there was the town I was born in—Ottawa, Illinois—a little bit bigger, but not much, and the same kind of people."

Phil soon found that making a deal in Walla Walla was quite a bit different than making a deal in the California wine country, or in Bordeaux.

"For us to come in from California and say we were interested in Washington state was a big deal for them. They welcomed you; they wanted you. The state government wanted to help you. Nobody was fighting you about this and that and the other thing. The enthusiasm and the excitement still exist up there. I found that and welcomed it. I really loved it."

The Canoe Ridge Vineyard is located about 100 miles slightly southwest of Walla Walla near Paterson, Washington. The 100-acre property overlooks the Columbia River from the north. When Chalone became involved in the venture, approximately 20 acres had been planted. The first order of business for the new partners was to raise the money necessary to plant out the rest of the property.

So where did they go to raise money in Walla Walla? The local bank? No, Phil, Chalone CFO Bill Hamilton and two of the Canoe Ridge partners went out to the Walla Walla Country Club.

"The four of us sat right off the 18th hole, and as a potential investor finished his round, one of the two partners would say, 'Hey, Joe, come on over here, we want to talk to you. Here's what we're planning to do, and these are the guys that are going to do it. You've heard of Chalone; we're going to make a bigger vineyard and then we're going to build a winery. If you want to continue to be my insurance guy, you'd better be interested.' And once some of the key people were behind it—and they already knew that Rick Small was getting into it—the others wanted to be a part of it. It was like Chalone all over again, except that instead of traveling all over the United States, we just traveled throughout Walla Walla helping our local partners raise the money."

151

However, it wasn't long before certain cultural differences between the local partners and Chalone began to surface.

Some of the partners who were farmers had a different view of the world than Rick Small, Dick Graff or Phil did. "After we started getting some grapes, one particular partner went out to the vineyard and saw that we were thinning the crop," Phil said. "He had a fit. He said, 'You're throwing money on the ground. You can't do this.' He would complain to the other farmers, who said, 'What do you mean you're throwing grapes on the ground?' 'Well, these are young vineyards,' Rick Small would say. 'You don't even take the grapes for the first five years.' That certainly didn't make them feel any better; and when we told them that the idea was to drop half the crop and make the other half for a second label or something like that, all of a sudden we found ourselves with a real problem with some of the partners."

Phil and his staff figured the situation could only get worse, since the partners on the vineyard side had a stake in the vineyard only. So anytime the crop was thinned, for example, the vineyard partners could claim that the value of their investment was being diminished to the benefit of Chalone and the winery side. The solution was elegant in concept yet complicated in execution: Phil decided that the vineyard partners should become partners in the winery side as well, thus sharing in the end product, the wine.

The question then became where to put the new winery. The original idea was to build the winery on the Canoe Ridge property near Paterson. Several logistical and other factors began to weigh in against that idea. "We decided to build the winery in Walla Walla. That's where a lot of the investors were, where all the people came to visit, and where you could hire people. There just wasn't anybody living out near Paterson. So we settled on Walla Walla and instead of building a winery, we leased the old Walla Walla Railway Engine House. It was an old brick building that, if it were located in California, wouldn't stand up to a magnitude 2 earthquake. It was huge, and everything was gone inside except the old tracks and gravel. Conveniently, the guy who owned it happened to be one of our partners."

Phil went to work with the Canoe Ridge partners to create a new winery company. Chalone would own 51 percent and the local vineyard partners would own 49 percent. The entire group, including Chalone, owned both the vineyard and the winery. Dick Graff sent Oregon native John Abbott up from Acacia to become the venture's winemaker. Canoe Ridge's first vintage was made at the Hyatt Vineyards winery up the road in Zillah, Washington, while management was working on the plans for the new winery. Canoe Ridge's second vintage was made at the Engine House winery.

"The incredible thing about eastern Washington—especially out in the area where Canoe Ridge is—is that we were the first and still are the only, to my knowledge, California winery that has ever made an investment up there. I think some people are just turned off about the risks and the weather, but it's just like anywhere else. You learn where to plant and what to plant and how the location demands that you do things differently. The huge advantage is that you can buy vineyard land for 10 percent of what you can buy it for here, with plenty of water," Phil said.

FOR CHALONE VINEYARD, the 1980s were a time of vineyard expansion. More than 40 acres of the former Creal property were planted. So were 26 more acres of Macwood. On the acres leased back to Chalone from the Pinnacles House property, there were an additional 10.5 acres planted. And Dick began putting in eight acres of vineyards on his personal property. All of this new grape production was destined for Chalone's wines.

While the 1980s was a decade of growth and momentum for Chalone, it was also a time of loss for the Graffs. In 1981 Lisa Graff, John's teenage daughter, died suddenly of respiratory failure. In 1988 Dick's mother, Estelle, died of cancer. Their ashes were buried at Chalone, on a hill that overlooks the vineyards and the winery. The spot is marked by a monument and a plaque for each.

16 | *Recession, War and Inklings of Battles to Come*

LOOKING BACK ON THE LAST DECADE, the 1980s had by any measure been a busy and extremely productive 10 years for the company. But as Chalone moved into the 1990s, Phil Woodward and Dick Graff couldn't possibly anticipate the challenges that lay ahead, especially while they were basking in the glow of a record year for sales and earnings in 1990.

The company decided to lead off the new decade by taking at least a symbolic step away from its increasingly corporate image by changing its name. Chalone Incorporated became Chalone Wine Group Ltd. "The word 'Incorporated' didn't give us the feeling that we wanted," Phil said. "Basically, we have an aversion to anything that has 'corporate' in it, and so the name Chalone, Incorporated became something we really didn't enjoy."

What was enjoyable was that Phil and Dick were at the helm of a growing stable of wineries, the more distant of which were a long way from the home office in San Francisco. They had a lot on their plates and a lot on their minds.

"Edna Valley was really taking off, and so was the whole Central Coast concept—which meant we weren't so unique anymore. So we needed to find ways to keep things growing there," Phil said. "We were also in the beginning of our expansion into Washington state. We were already selling Woodward Canyon wines, and our Canoe Ridge venture was getting off the ground. We were the first and only California wine company to make an investment there—so that was new and exciting. The other thing was Carmenet. Carmenet was still trying to find its niche, its identity, so that was somewhat of a worry, and I was forced to take a real hard look at that."

Carmenet had always been something of a problem child for Chalone. Because of the way the company acquired Carmenet—a project well underway that fell into tough financial times, they inherited much that they could not change. The high cost of the winery alone, for example, was not the Chalone style, and it took years before that winery could be finished. The bottom line for Phil was that they had invested a lot of money for a small-production brand. And although Carmenet was making a little bit of money, Phil felt it wasn't pulling its weight.

"Clearly, something had to be done. So, I decided to move Mike Richmond from National Sales Manager to be Carmenet's General Manager to work with Jeff Baker. What Carmenet needed was a personality, somebody who had the imagination to make something happen. I felt Mike could do that. And Robert Farver was fast becoming a guy who could be our VP of sales going forward. So when Mike went to Carmenet, he and Jeff got along very well. They started making changes that needed to be made, and part of that was the Dynamite Cabernet concept, which really, really turned that place around; the two of them created a whole new product line," Phil said.

The Dynamite Cabernet program grew so quickly, in fact, that while initially Jeff Baker was able to make the wine at Carmenet, it soon became necessary to make some of it at Acacia. It became clear to everyone that if the growth was going to continue, they would need to find another facility to produce it.

1991 STARTED OFF IN A VERY UNUSUAL MANNER. A crisis called the Gulf War happened. And with that came the beginning of a very rough period for the company.

"The whole industry experienced a slowdown in sales, and we were no exception," Phil said. "Unfortunately, we were also saddled with a lot more debt than we should have had. The interest on that debt was killing us. Sales started to slow down but the interest was still there. We made a little bit of money that year, but it wasn't much.

"You know, 1991 was one of those years—the Gulf War was going on, but you didn't realize how badly it was affecting you. You just kept saying, 'Well, this isn't going to last,' but it did. Looking back on it with all the money we borrowed for expansion, we were just trapped in between too, too much debt and falling sales. We just didn't think it was going to keep going."

There was a brief ray of sunshine for Phil and the company in the form of the first harvest at the Canoe Ridge project up in Washington state. The drought that had been a problem in the area seemed to be going away, and that first vintage was good in terms of quality. However, that ray of sunshine was quickly eclipsed by a dark cloud in the form of a crisis that would shake the foundations of nearly 20 years of partnership.

Richard Graff, co-founder of the modern Chalone Vineyard and co-founder of the Chalone Wine Group, was losing interest in the business he had worked so hard to help build. Phil Woodward, his partner since 1972, was more worried about that than the Gulf War and the recession combined.

"It had been a small concern of mine and of the board in the 1980s, especially with Dick's co-founding and growing role with the American Institute of Wine & Food," Phil said. "But by the early '90s it had become a much bigger issue. In many ways, Dick was just being Dick. I mean, he had all these interests from philosophy to music to food and wine, and he had made the decision that he just wasn't going to spend 100 percent of his time on Chalone. That was a real disappointment to me, because the two of us had been great partners for so long. I felt that he could do his other interests away from Chalone, that they wouldn't interfere with his responsibilities at the company, which was overseeing all the grape growing and all the winemaking. Key responsibilities. But it became increasingly clear that he was ignoring those responsibilities. I still had a great respect for him, but he just wasn't there, especially at this critical time. I talked with him about it and he basically told me, 'I have all these other interests, but I can do it. It doesn't make any difference how much time I spend on it, it's the quality that comes out of it; quality of time versus quantity.'"

The evidence that Dick's "quality vs. quantity" argument wasn't bearing out could be seen in the most important of all measures: the quality of the company's wines.

"We first saw the problem at Chalone. The wines in the mid to late 1980s were not up to standards. Dick wasn't paying enough attention, and, while Mike Michaud was there, he wasn't yet capable of making the wines that Dick had been making. Edna Valley experienced problems, too. A lot of it had to do with the fact that Dick wasn't going down there. The winemaker at the time, again, didn't have the ability—the technical ability and sometimes the management ability to run that operation. Our partners in Edna Valley, the Nivens, could see it, and they were not happy about it either," Phil said. "Acacia and Carmenet weren't affected as much because both Larry Brooks and Jeff Baker were experienced winemakers—they were used to running the show on their own. And having Mike Richmond at Carmenet helped a lot, too."

This situation is clearly not easy for Phil to reflect on or to talk about. It was also not an easy issue to discuss at the board of directors level—many of the directors, because of their long friendships and loyalty to both Dick and Phil, simply did not want to recognize what was happening. It was not until the Rothschilds and the Hojels became involved with the company and the board, as pure outsiders, that pressure was applied to deal with the situation.

"Especially in light of the way things were trending, namely, down, both the Rothschilds and the Hojels joined me in saying that we had to make a change," Phil said. "One of us had to be totally in charge. The splitting of responsibilities wasn't working anymore and the board decided that Dick would step aside from his day-to-day management of the production side of the business. He would still remain chairman, but not any more than that."

The year was 1992 and things were not looking good. Sales were not increasing as planned, and now, with a clear mandate from the board, Phil started making some changes.

"We had too much debt, we had too much overhead and we had to start making some real decisions on what to do about that. It was clear that we were going to have to find a way to jump-start sales, and we had to find a way to reduce the debt load. Also, by this time, it was pretty clear that the way we structured the deal with the Rothschilds wasn't working. The partnership was fine, but the cross-investment wasn't working. We were paying all this interest and we weren't getting much back in dividends; and the stock price wasn't going up so we couldn't convert the debentures, even if we wanted to call them. So it was time to try to reassess that relationship. Those things don't happen overnight. It took a couple of years to try to get that one to the point where we needed to be. We also started talking about having to raise some more money," Phil said.

But Phil's biggest problem in many ways was that he was now in charge of production at the company's wineries. He's the first to admit that he wasn't a production person and that he couldn't have the winemakers reporting to him for long.

"I had to find the person I could trust and work with and who really had the ability to oversee all the production. So in 1993 I named Larry Brooks to take over the responsibility. I thought he was the logical person," Phil said.

But as 1993 came and went without much improvement and, in fact, another net loss, the board—especially the larger shareholders—started to wonder whether Phil was the right person to turn the company around or if they should consider bringing someone else in.

Phil was sure that he could do it. He had specific ideas and a plan to turn the company around, and, as long as he had the total power to make things happen, he would turn it around. The decision was made to give Phil a shot at it, but the Rothschilds wanted an executive committee formed to help manage the company through the crisis.

The executive committee was to be made up of five members of the board, and Richard Hojel was to be the chairman of the committee. Phil, as the president and CEO, reported to the committee weekly on his activities and progress.

Phil began to implement his turnaround plan. His first steps? "I had to cut salaries, and I volunteered to be the first. I took a significant cut in salary and then insisted that everyone else at the top do the same. I then introduced the Morro Bay Chardonnay with the idea of getting some quick sales there. Then I had to eliminate some jobs; that was something we'd never had to do before," Phil said.

How did employees react to these changes? According to Phil, everyone knew that the company was in trouble. The company still had a "family" culture, and, because it was Phil making the cuts and not some "hired guns," morale seemed to stay on the upside.

"I asked people to take cuts in salary rather than let them go," Phil said. "I told them, 'Take a 20 percent cut, or a 10 percent cut, and rather than eliminate your job, we'll turn this thing around and you'll get the pay cut back. Forget bonuses for a while, but we'll get some stock options.' That's what happened. The fact was that everyone felt this was still a family; we were going to come out of this together. It was amazing the cooperation I got."

1993 TURNED OUT TO BE ANOTHER VERY TOUGH YEAR for the company. In fact, its end marked seven straight quarters of red ink. It was so tough that Phil decided to eliminate the fancy annual report altogether, to just write a cover letter on top of the 10K annual report that they were required to file with the SEC and to send that out to shareholders.

It was also the year that the company decided to leave its home of 20 years, San Francisco, and move north to the Napa Valley.

"The major reason behind the move was the warehouse," Phil said. "We had a rented warehouse in Sonoma and a warehouse in the City. But ideally, we really wanted the headquarters and the warehouse in one spot. To do that you needed a place where the trucks could get in and out. And as you grew, you needed space to expand both the offices and the warehouse. We looked at ways to do that in San Francisco, but when you really think about it, the big 18-wheelers don't like coming into San Francisco anyway—they want easy access. So when the earthquake hit in 1989—thank God we were all out of the building, because we were in an old brick building and the top floor just caved in—we never went back. We had to go in another building temporarily. So we were in disarray there and trying to find another location, which we finally did. But the space was much more expensive, and San Francisco has a payroll tax, along with other disincentives, like no parking. We said, 'Who needs this?' Sonoma was the first choice, but there was no office space to speak of there. Bill Hamilton was in charge of all this, and he found the park in Napa which had only two buildings in it at the time. Times were still tough, and people were doing anything to get you to sign a lease, so we got a really good deal to come here."

The move meant a longer commute for Phil and others in the company. Some decided to move north. The move made a tremendous amount of sense on paper, and, at the time, that was important. Phil knew that they would lose some employees, but not the key ones.

All through this period of cost cutting and bad times, Phil was learning a lot about Chalone as a business, and a lot about himself.

"It taught me that with a company as small as we were, if you get yourself in too much debt, you're asking for trouble. Just the slightest downturn in sales can really turn things upside down fast. That debt is a fixed expense, and to try to compensate for it by cutting certain things doesn't give you much to go on. There aren't that many fixed expenses in this business that you can cut, and you don't want to cut the things that are going to make your wine suffer in quality. It's not as though you're going to stop using barrels; you just couldn't do that. The other thing that I learned is that from the standpoint of morale, it's amazing that people will take a hit financially if the head guy does it too, and if they think they're going to get it back. They don't want to leave the company, they want to believe in it," Phil said.

The other thing Phil learned was that Chalone's multiwinery approach was proving itself out as a valid business model. The company didn't have all of its eggs in one basket; it had several brands each with its own defined market niche. This diversification helped the company when times were tough, or, when one particular brand or niche wasn't doing so well, the others were there to shoulder the load.

Almost unnoticed in all the turmoil of the early 1990s was the 20th anniversary of Phil Woodward's first day with Chalone. Some in his position, in charge and responsible for turning around a nearly $20 million company, would have decided that it was time to move on.

"No, never. I was married to this company, and the passion was so strong that I never even considered it," Phil said. "The challenge was there for me to turn it around, but to ask somebody else to do it? No. I'd never be able to live with myself. I felt that I wanted to do this; I could do it; once I got it done, then it was time to find somebody else because it was no longer a bootstrap operation. It was no longer just a club of a few people who put this thing together. It wasn't just an entrepreneurial thing anymore. It was really becoming a large enough business that neither Dick nor I should be there running it day to day. With the outside influences of the Rothschilds and Hojels, it was clearly a different company from the one Dick and I had started. But personally I had no interest in leaving, and personally I really wanted to make this a profitable company again."

17 | *A Strong Comeback*

THE COMPANY'S EFFORTS AT COST CUTTING, restructuring and increasing sales would continue through 1994. Progress had indeed been made and it looked like there was a glimmer of light at the end of the tunnel. Sales were picking up as well, so Phil turned his attention to the serious financial restructuring that remained unfinished.

That restructuring took two forms. First, there was a private placement among several of the existing major shareholders to raise money for paying down the debt that continued to plague the company. The second part of the restructuring had to do with the company's cross ownership in Domaines Barons de Rothschild (DBR).

"Our idea was to change the arrangement from having an ownership interest in DBR that paid a cash dividend into an arrangement wherein we owned one of their wine properties with them, and shared in that particular property's success," Phil said. "We knew that Château Lafite was off limits. We weren't really interested in buying into Château Rieussec or getting involved in Chile; so Château Duhart-Milon was the logical choice. DBR owned 100 percent of it and the wines were ones that we could sell more of than anything else. It took some negotiating, but they finally came around and agreed to do it. In retrospect, it's turned out to be one of the best things we've ever done. It's a wonderful property that throws off a lot of cash because it's very profitable and there isn't any debt."

Controlling costs became a mission for Phil. In developing his turn-around plan for the company, he had set certain cost-cutting goals for the company and himself to achieve. In 1994, he hit the one benchmark he felt was most important: getting his sales, general and administrative costs (SG&A) down to 20 percent of sales. In 1994, he hit 21 percent.

"It really did become a mission on my part," Phil said. "Part of that is my accounting background, I guess, because I measure things like that. But when you're in charge of turning around a company, you've got to have some benchmarks to measure against. That was one of my goals: to take the SG&A down to 20 percent of sales, with the idea that we could have an operating profit that would be 20 percent as well."

The fact that all of these steps began to show results in 1994 made the accountant in Phil feel pretty good. Having the mandate to turn the company around; being able to set goals and make the decisions and take the steps necessary to achieve them; and then to be able to measure the impact of those efforts fueled his confidence in the steps he was taking and his drive to continue the mission.

"It really did feel great. It was just me with the help of people like Larry Brooks, Bill Hamilton and Robert Farver," Phil said. "I just started making decisions—boom, boom, boom. By getting some short-term reporting back to me on a weekly basis, I reported to the board every month what we were doing. When you begin to see the results, it's a good feeling. During all this time, Richard Hojel was the head of the executive committee. He was a big supporter of mine, and that support was very important. He gave me every reason to believe that I could do it."

Phil also thought that the company's ability to move toward the goals he and the executive committee were setting, not the least of which was the 20 percent SG&A goal, seemed to again reaffirm the original multiple winery-one management concept.

"I remember that a lot of people felt our strategy was wrong because it wasn't efficient on the production side; but my background told me that we could afford to be a little less efficient at that end if we could get high enough prices for our wines, because smaller production would translate into higher quality, which translated into higher prices," Phil said.

Even more importantly, Phil felt that if you had these multiple wineries under one roof, sharing the "overhead"—the selling costs, the distribution costs, the marketing costs and the administrative costs—that is where you could really make your efficiency count.

And as the economy began to rebound late in 1994, the company took advantage of those efficiencies to score a strong increase in sales—up to $21 million. Phil and everyone at the company, from the directors to the cellar workers, hoped that a new upward trend was taking hold.

WHILE 1995 ENDED UP BEING ANOTHER GOOD YEAR from the standpoint of sales and earnings, and the finalization of the restructured cross-ownership with DBR, the year ended on a tragic note.

Richard Hojel, the patriarch of the Mexico City-based family that had become a major investor in the company, died in November. Richard, who was a director and the chairman of the executive committee, also served a very important role as a facilitator and consensus builder between the company and its French shareholders. He was also a friend and close advisor to Phil Woodward.

"Richard's death really was a blow," Phil said. "Not only was he a great guy, but he was able to bridge the American way of doing business and the European way of doing business. There were some definite differences of opinion between the French and us, and he was able to sit in the middle and talk to both sides and help bridge that gap of differences."

Richard Hojel's death created a critical void in the balance of leadership between the French shareholders and the company's American management. Christophe Salin, president of DBR, was named to head the executive committee to continue Richard's work in helping Phil rebuild the company.

Richard's son, Mark Hojel, came on the board to take his father's place as a director. Mark, currently the president of the Monte Xanic winery in Baja California, was a very young man when he came to the Chalone board.

"Mark is the same age as my son Scott, who is one of our top senior regional sales managers," Phil said. "Mark was a recent graduate of UCLA Business School, where I was involved with him on doing his thesis on the wine business. He's a very intelligent guy and he's grown to like this business a lot. I remember talking to Richard before he died about his plan to have Mark come on the board. He didn't think he was quite ready for it, but he was clearly going in that direction. So it just happened sooner rather than later."

THE YEAR 1996 goes down in the history of the Chalone Wine Group as a year of milestones and extreme events.

Financially, it was the most successful year in the company's history. Sales jumped to an all-time high of $31 million, while net profits soared to $2.3 million. Clearly the turnaround efforts had produced some significant results. In addition, the economy was really picking up speed. That upturn allowed the company to raise some prices and sell wines through a lot faster.

And Phil had actually beat his key benchmark of bringing sales, general and administrative expenses down to 20 percent of sales. "We hit 19 percent! You know, I guess 1996 was really the year that the turnaround had been accomplished," Phil said. "Now if the need arose, I could begin to think about finding a replacement for me who could take on a really healthy company, rather than one in trouble. It meant a lot to me, personally, to be in a position to hand it off to somebody in good shape."

Other benchmarks and extreme events for 1996: it was the year of the raging wildland fire that swept over and around the Carmenet winery. It was the year that Chalone hit 12,000 shareholders, up from 300 at the time the company went public just over 11 years before. And it was the first year in nearly 25 years that Richard Graff's name did not appear on the Letter to Shareholders in the company's 1996 annual report.

By this time, Dick's role at the company had seriously diminished. He was still technically the chairman of the board of directors, but his day-to-day involvement in the company's management was non-existent and he had sold almost all of his company stock. Because of this, and as a culmination of Dick's removal from day-to-day management beginning back in 1992, there was clearly a movement on the board to remove him from the company completely. And that's what happened.

There was no public announcement that Dick was officially leaving the company. In fact, the public perception was that he was still actively involved.

And on reflection, Phil felt only sadness that his long-time friend, partner and co-founder was no longer a part of the company that he had helped build.

IT WAS JULY 31, 1996, and residents of Sonoma Valley went about the business of daily life in their bucolic "Valley of the Moon." Early in the afternoon, some paused to look at a small, rising plume of smoke emanating from the hills northwest of the town of Sonoma.

It wasn't long before that plume of smoke became a raging wildfire, plainly visible to all in the valley as it raced up a canyon and over hills driven by high temperatures, low humidity and hot, summer winds. The Cavedale fire started when power lines arced as they hit a tree during the windy afternoon. The fire charred 2,127 acres before more than 1,000 firefighters brought it under control.

Among those acres burned were 95 belonging to Carmenet, which sat right in the path of the raging inferno.

"I was in my car coming back from Chalone and I heard it on the news—it didn't say Carmenet, but I sure as hell knew it was close to where we were," Phil said. "The fire was pretty far away from us when it first started, so when the wind shifted and came across and then came roaring down our canyon, Mike Richmond, who was in charge of the winery at the time, told everybody to go home except for three or four, and they manned the hoses. The idea was to try to save the winery, because there wasn't anything else you could do. Nobody was coming up—no fire personnel or anything like that. And so they just watered down the roofs because it's all redwood and shake shingles—and the fire just went right around them. Jeff Baker, our winemaker who lives on the mountain, lost part of his house, but we didn't lose any part of the winery. I mean those guys really saved it. They were heroes. If it had caught, it would have gone up in a minute.

"But we did lose about 60 percent of the vineyard. They say a vineyard can't burn, but what happened was that the grasses in the vineyard, which we use for erosion control, had not been cut as low as maybe they should have been. But that's not important because it was a firestorm and it came roaring through and caught the grasses on fire, caught the stakes on fire, even the plastic drip irrigation burned. We were able to stop it—or it stopped itself. It didn't leap over to another section of our vineyard, but the burned vines were essentially destroyed."

One could wonder whether Phil and others at Chalone would think there was some kind of jinx associated with Carmenet. It took so long to get up and running, so many obstacles and roadblocks over the years keeping it from hitting critical mass. Phil dismisses that idea out of hand.

"The fire and losing the vineyard didn't make me feel it was jinxed at all. It's just another one of those things that happen when you're building a company or running a company—you just say, 'Damn.' But if the company had been made up of only Carmenet, it would have been a disaster. But being part of a portfolio of wineries, the company sailed right on through it. But thank God nobody was hurt," Phil said.

IF 1996 WAS A YEAR OF EXTREME UPS AND DOWNS, 1997 was a year that the company took a collective breath and started to look to the future.

It was a time of continuing adjustments and tweaking by Phil to continue the recovery process and get the company on a steady upward growth curve. He would succeed, driving the Chalone Wine Group to a sales record of $36 million. One of those tweaks seemed insignificant, almost trivial, but it actually was the kind of organizational change that can ripple positively throughout a company.

"We changed our fiscal year from one based on the calendar year to one ending March 31," Phil said. "We had been talking about this for years. Having a year-end coincide with the calendar makes for a crazy time, because you're trying to budget the next year before December 31, and yet all the sales people are still going nuts trying to make the current year come together. The last thing I wanted to do was worry about budgeting work during that period. A close on March 31 gives us the advantage of doing the budget process in a period when there's a little bit more down time."

The company was also embarking on an ambitious new expansion of the winery facilities at Edna Valley. "Little did we ever guess that this little 25,000-case winery would someday be expanded to produce 150,000 cases of wine," Phil said.

In December 1997, Michael Michaud left his position as Chalone Vineyard's winemaker to make wine under his own label from his own vineyards on the Chalone benchland. Dan Karlsen, Chalone's current winemaker, came on board in early 1998.

At the board level, a much more far-reaching discussion about the future of Chalone Wine Group was taking place. The question was: Who will lead us into the new millennium?

"I had conversations with some of the board members and eventually with all of them. It was clear that if we were going to take the company to the next level, which to us was $100 million in sales, it was going to take a different type of person than me. I consider myself more of an entrepreneurial type—get things started and financed and get people going—but I don't consider myself a professional manager. I'm really good at doing certain things—motivating people and getting people to buy into strategies and cultures—but when you're getting up to $50 million in sales and shooting for $100 million, you've got a different ballgame altogether. Not only were there others who could do the job better, I was pretty sure that I simply didn't want to do it," Phil said.

The result of this discussion was that the board agreed with Phil and gave him one year to find his replacement. Phil began immediately to talk to the company's accountants, attorneys and other advisors looking for candidates. Between them Phil was able to come up with approximately a dozen names that he considered good candidates. He contacted all of them, and six agreed that they would like to be considered for the position of president. Phil interviewed those six and narrowed down the list to three top candidates.

"I told the board that I would bring them three candidates," Phil said. "A committee of the board could then interview them and we, together, would make the final decision. I thought to myself, I wanted an outside executive recruiter to have a shot at finding some candidates."

Phil contacted the recruiter, Hank Teahan of Gorlick and Associates, and gave him the names of the people he had already talked to—they were off limits. He gave the recruiter 30 days to come up with some new names. Teahan came back with several new names, one of them Tom Selfridge, then a senior executive at Kendall-Jackson Winery. Phil was surprised.

"I never thought about Tom ever being interested. He never came up on anybody's charts, anybody's radar screens. I told Hank to contact him and see what his interest level was, and Tom told him he wasn't interested," Phil said. "We were both disappointed, because we thought he would have made a good candidate. Meanwhile, Hank had given me some other names. I interviewed two of them and one was pretty good."

While Phil continued to refine his search, Tom Selfridge told his wife, Robin, about the recruiter's call. She said, "Are you crazy? You really ought to at least talk to him." Tom called Hank and told him that he had reconsidered.

"Hank called me back in the middle of the night at home to tell me this," Phil said. "I find out that Tom also lives in Marin, and we arranged to have breakfast. I could tell an hour into this 'breakfast interview' that Tom was going to be a real strong candidate. The more I met with him, the more I felt that way.

"At this time, I hadn't involved anybody else from the company in this process, but as Tom came to the top, especially with his background in production, I could see that it might conflict with what Larry Brooks was doing. I really didn't want to lose Larry—he had been my right-hand guy through the tough times. I wanted him to interview Tom because if he felt comfortable with it, then that would be a real positive. Larry interviewed him, and he came to me and said, 'This guy is really great. He'd be a great president.'"

Phil was satisfied that he had found his three candidates. He submitted them to the board's search committee, which included Baron Eric de Rothschild, and the next step was for the search committee to interview the final three. The committee unanimously chose Tom Selfridge to be the next president of the Chalone Wine Group. Tom would join the company officially January 1, 1998, after taking a couple of months off between Kendall-Jackson and Chalone.

Phil would remain as CEO and chairman of the company, but clearly the baton had been passed. The company had found its day-to-day leader for the new millennium in Tom Selfridge. How did Phil feel about handing over the reigns?

"A lot of people have asked me that. It would have been hard for me to turn it over to somebody who wasn't my choice. But when you make the choice and it doesn't work out—and I'm sure the search committee had this in mind—then you have only yourself to blame. If you make the choice and it does work out, then it feels great. It's worked out extremely well. I'm doing what I really want to do now, and I'm not doing what I don't want to do," Phil said.

18 | *A Terrible Accident*

EVEN AS PLANS WERE PROGRESSING to position the Chalone Wine Group for dramatic growth and development into the future, certain aspects of the past weighed heavily on Phil Woodward.

Phil's role in the company was changing dramatically. He was relinquishing the role of day-to-day manager as president and CEO while embracing the long-range, big-picture role of chairman. And he was happy about the changes. But increasingly his thoughts returned to still-fresh and unhappy memories of how his partnership with Richard Graff had ended.

"I have to admit that I was hurt and I was upset," Phil said. "I devoted almost my whole adult business life to this company, and to watch my partner, who, quite frankly, for a long time was getting paid as much as I was and not spending as much time as I was, it upset me. I would talk to him at certain times about it, and his answer always was, 'It doesn't make any difference how many hours you put in, it's what you do.' The bottom line from our conversations about it was that Dick wasn't going to change. So when it came time to not pay him anymore and move him out, he didn't resist. The company bought his house and vineyard on the Chalone benchland so Dick had some money. The deal allowed Dick to live at the house for the rest of his life. A couple of times I got really mad

at him and told him, 'You know, you let us down—you left us.' The relationship deteriorated in the last few years. It didn't mean that I still did-
n't have a lot of respect for him, and he for me. When we would disagree
at board meetings, Dick would be the first to say, 'Don't think because
Phil and I disagree on this point that we don't have a lot of mutual
respect for one another. I don't want to give the impression that our relationship is some superficial thing; it's not.' And I believe that. It was certainly true on my part."

Phil clearly wanted to do something to try to repair the rift—to repair
his friendship with Dick. He didn't know how to go about it and at
times felt the conflict between his desire to do so and his growing frus-
tration with the public perception that Dick was still running the show
at Chalone.

And clearly that perception was out there. Whether innocent media
mistakes or somehow encouraged by Dick, references to him in the
media, and one publication in particular, as late as January 1998 identi-
fied him as the chairman of the Chalone Wine Group, even after the hiring of Tom Selfridge and the elevation of Phil to chairman had been
announced and publicized by the same publication.

"You know, it really never bothered me during the first 10 or 15 years,
because one of the things that brought us together was our comple-
mentary skills," Phil said. "I couldn't cover the production side of it. It
didn't bother me in those years at all. I don't have an ego that needs pub-
licity. I wanted him to get out more. But honestly, during the last 10
years, it did begin to bother me. As the CEO of the company, I was clearly the guy who was driving the company, and yet some people still
thought and wrote as if he was involved."

One article was particularly painful and really made Phil question
Dick's motives, as well as his own desire to somehow reconcile at least
his friendship with Dick. The article, a column by *Wine Spectator* Senior
Editor James Laube, ran under the headline "Changes at Chalone Might
Do Some Good" and appeared in the January 31, 1998, issue of the mag-
azine. The column was generally critical of the company and its man-

agement, including newly hired president Tom Selfridge, claiming among other things that the company "has been in dire need of leadership, direction and new products for some time," and that "Chalone Wine Group seems to have been in a trance for a decade." Most frustrating to Phil was a comment attributed to Dick:

Richard Graff, cwg's chairman, admits the company has been plagued by what he termed "inertia" and that cwg "has been dragging its feet" by not making more innovative or affordable wines.

At approximately 6 p.m. on January 9, 1998, Richard Graff was flying alone in his single-engine Cessna aircraft south toward Soledad, on his way back to his home on the benchland near Chalone. When the plane began to lose power, he attempted to turn the plane around and make an emergency landing at the Salinas airport. He didn't make it. The plane crashed into a power pole and then into a greenhouse, bursting into flames. He was killed instantly.

"That was a night I will never forget," Phil said. "I was in Los Angeles and my wife called me at about 10:30 that night. The authorities had finally been able to identify Dick and they sent somebody from the Sheriff's Office to Chalone. They found a light on at Rich Boer's house—our vineyard manager—and they told him. Rich called me at home. I wasn't there, and my wife answered the phone. That one was a real tough one to take. I was devastated."

More than 300 people attended Dick's memorial service at Grace Cathedral in San Francisco. Phil gave one of the eulogies, relating his 27 years with Dick Graff—the winemaker, cook, writer, philosopher, musician and pilot.

19 | *Getting Ready for the Millennium*

THE FIRST BRAND THAT NEWLY HIRED PRESIDENT TOM SELFRIDGE took on at Chalone was what would become Echelon. Tom took a good initial idea, found its flaws and made it a winner.

"Echelon has its roots with our Morro Bay program," Phil said. "The problem with Morro Bay was that I was too anxious to get results fast, and it became just another private label. We needed to do something at the $10 per bottle price point, and it was generally agreed that our effort there should really have its own brand identity, as opposed to being a second label for one of the wineries."

Prior to this time, the general consensus had been that each of the wineries should have its own second label. The company's French directors were the first to propose that instead of all those second labels, why not create one winery and brand in that lower price point that all of the other wineries contributed to. For some time, Phil and his team just could not figure out how to execute that idea.

"The best idea we came up with was a plan Larry Brooks and I developed," Phil said. "We were going to build this huge facility to make the wines, and all the grapes were going to come from vineyards in Clarksburg, which was then owned by the Meyers family, who were also on our board. We proposed to the board that this was going to become our new line of wines at the $10 price point."

"Tom was able to find rented facilities to make the wines for the new line including grapes from the Clarksburg vineyard. The original concept called for two wines, a Chardonnay and a Syrah, but Tom, with all his experience in where to find grapes and bulk wines, and Larry, put together a Pinot Noir and Merlot as well."

During the time that they were developing and executing the concept that would become Echelon, steps were taken to eliminate all of the existing second labels at each winery. This was done to make sure that Echelon would have a clear niche at its price point without any internal competition—there would be enough external competition to worry about. The next big decision was what to call the new brand.

"Mike Richmond came up with the name of Echelon," Phil said. "Before, I probably would have sat on it and had everybody in the company thinking about it for days or weeks. We all looked at it and said, 'That sounds good.' Tom said, 'OK, that's it,' and a brand was born. Echelon never would have happened without Tom Selfridge. He knew what to do and how to do it."

Meanwhile, up at Carmenet, two projects were in the works to continue the steady gains in sales and profitability there through the 1990s.

First, desperately in need of space to expand Carmenet's production capacity in light of the growing success of the Dynamite line of wines, the company acquired the Vintage Lane property in Glen Ellen on the Sonoma Valley floor. The property was the home of the former Grand Cru winery and was owned at the time by Associated Vintners. Negotiations had gone on for some time, until finally in March of 1998 agreement was reached. Plans for production and barrel storage space are currently under development.

The second project was the two-year-old settlement talks with Pacific Gas & Electric Company over damage to the Carmenet vineyards from the 1996 Cavedale fire.

"Those were just terrible negotiations," Phil said. "Our CFO, Bill Hamilton, and our attorneys did most of it. PG&E was just really, really difficult to deal with. In the end, after Tom came on board, we finally just said to our attorneys, 'We have to settle this thing. It's been two years, three years almost.' They had already admitted it was their fault, and after the parade of experts on each side, they said they'd pay us $1 million. We said we wanted $18 million. In the end, we reached a settlement for $5 million. Interestingly, that's the exact number that Hamilton and I both answered one month after the fire to the question 'What would we take today to settle?' That was the number we said, and that's the number we got three years later."

Up in Washington state, the company's Canoe Ridge venture was booming. The vineyard overlooking the Columbia River near Paterson, Washington, had been fully planted to Chardonnay, Merlot and some Cabernet Sauvignon. The vineyard would be able to supply enough fruit for a 35,000-case production. One hundred miles away, in Walla Walla, the Canoe Ridge winery—located in the old railroad engine house—was producing about 25,000 cases of estate-grown wines. The winery couldn't handle the 35,000-case production of the vineyard, and so the decision facing Phil and Tom was whether they should expand the engine house winery, sell and move on, or build another facility somewhere else. They decided to purchase two lots adjacent to the winery and expand the facility, adding additional winery capacity as well as a barrel storage facility.

"Canoe Ridge has been profitable from the first year. Recently we tried to make an offer to buy out our limited partners, and they wouldn't even think of it," Phil said. "They just say, 'There isn't a price high enough.' They're making a lot of money and they're having a lot of fun. And so are we."

As promising as the future for Canoe Ridge Vineyard looked, it was only the beginning of the company's investment in the future of Washington state wines.

WHAT DOES A CALIFORNIA-BASED WINE COMPANY with 40 percent French ownership see in investing in eastern Washington state?

Potential. The future. And the past.

"Our initial plan in Washington for Canoe Ridge Vineyard was that it would be the Chalone Vineyard of Washington state for us," Phil said. "We want to keep it as a nearly 100-percent estate-bottled, higher-priced, limited-production brand. What's happening in Walla Walla is exactly what I thought would happen. It is becoming the nucleus of some really high-end wineries, and now everybody wants to be there. I believe that Walla Walla is and will continue to develop as the Napa Valley of Washington state."

Because of his belief in the future of Washington state, Phil and Tom started to explore ways that they could get involved in other projects up there. And while the structure of Canoe Ridge initially as a partnership with local investors made sense as a means of introduction and statement of good intentions from an "interloping" California company, things were different in the late 1990s. Chalone now had the knowledge of the area as well as the financial wherewithal to start a new project on its own.

So Phil decided to step up his efforts to find a second venture in Washington about the same time that Tom joined the company.

"Unfortunately, Tom didn't know anything about Washington state at the time," Phil said. "He said he'd been up there once with Jess Jackson; they looked around for one day and somebody said, 'Well you get a freeze once every 10 years.' Jess said, 'Forget it; I'm out of here.' That was the extent of Tom's exposure to Washington state. He knew more about Argentina and Chile. When he came on board and saw what we were doing up there and got to really know a lot more of what was going on in Washington, he got as excited as me. So together we felt, OK, let's go and find something else."

Because Chalone had developed such good relationships with grow-ers in eastern Washington—especially those in and around Walla Walla, most of whom were shareholders—it was not a huge project to lock in some contracts for Cabernet Sauvignon and Merlot. With those kinds of contracts, it was simply a matter of figuring out where they were going to make the wines, what were they going to call the new brand, and how it would be positioned in the marketplace.

"First we made an offer to buy The Hogue Cellars in Prosser; that didn't work out. Then Hogue came back and wanted to do a joint venture, but we didn't want to do that. Then we were looking around for a place to build a winery, and Staton Hills in Yakima became available. I had looked at Staton Hills about three years before, but it just didn't make sense for us at that time. Now the opportunity came back at a much lower price, and owned by a Japanese Pepsi-Cola bottler who was looking for a way out. We were able to work a deal with them to buy it," Phil said.

The company purchased the Staton Hills winery—the facility and the inventory—for $6 million in June of 1999.

"Clearly, we didn't buy Staton Hills because the wine was great; it's not," Phil said. "But it's a beautiful facility; it's a large facility. It's built so we can make 40,000 to 50,000 cases right now—and it's the first winery you see when you come over the interstate from Seattle. That fact didn't escape us. More and more people go over there for the weekend, buy their wines, and go back. So even without trying, the former owners were doing $250,000 of sales in this tasting room with wine that really was not that good."

As the company took over the operation, the first step was to bring in a new general manager and winemaker. Kevin Mott, who at the time was leaving his post after more than 10 years as winemaker and general manager at Idaho's Ste. Chapelle winery had been offered a position as head winemaker at Chateau Ste. Michelle, Washington state's largest winery. Mott was considering that position when recruiter Hank Teahan called Tom to let him know that Mott might be the perfect person for the Staton Hills job. As they learned of Mott's experience with eastern Washington grapes and winemaking, Phil and Tom didn't waste any time.

"Tom talked to Kevin Mott and we flew him down to Napa for the weekend. He signed with us that Monday," Phil said.

Next on the list was coming up with a name for the new winery. Phil and Tom had no interest in the name Staton Hills. The reputation it carried was not good. So it was back to the drawing boards.

"I was in Seattle with Tom while we were doing the deal for Staton Hills and, as usual, I was in a bookstore looking around," Phil said. "I noticed a book there called 'East of the Mountains' by David Guterson, the author of 'Snow Falling on Cedars.' It was about the area near the Yakima Valley where Staton Hills was located. So I got the book and started reading through a part of it. In the first chapter, he describes the area where we are, and part of it talks about the hay fields, vineyards, apple orchards and sagelands. Next, we had Debbie Joseph, Tom's executive assistant, do some research on the Internet on the history of the area. Part of what she found was about the Yakima Indians. One of the sub-tribes of the Yakimas that lived in the area around the winery was called the 'sagebrush people,' and the area around the winery was called the 'sage plains.' So Tom and Debbie and I started throwing around the theme and came up with Sagelands. I talked to a few other people like Robert Farver, and they thought it sounded good. So that's it. The Sagelands brand was born."

The concept for the Sagelands brand is to be the Edna Valley to Canoe Ridge's Chalone. The idea is for a brand that produces all red wines—Cabernet Sauvignon and Merlot—and the price point will be around $15 per bottle. The first release under the new Sagelands label will be the 1998 vintage.

ON FEBRUARY 2, 2000, THE COMPANY MADE AN ANNOUNCEMENT that in many ways was a culmination of a long quest for Phil Woodward.

For years, Phil knew that the one thing missing from the Chalone Wine Group's stable of brands and wineries was an ultra-premium Napa Valley Cabernet Sauvignon. For years he kept his eyes and ears open for the right opportunity—whether that was acquiring an existing brand

and property, or a prestigious vineyard, and building the brand and the wine from scratch. No workable opportunities presented themselves.

With Tom Selfridge on board, however, all that could now change.

Tom's background prior to joining Kendall Jackson was at Beaulieu Vineyard in Rutherford—the heart of Napa Valley's "Cabernet Country." He worked as BV's winemaker for 10 years before becoming the winery's president.

Thus, when the opportunity presented itself to purchase the Hewitt Ranch, a 69-acre property located just northwest of Beaulieu on the west side of Highway 29, Tom didn't have to do very much homework to figure out that it would be a win-win for the company. He was very familiar with the property's 57-acre Cabernet Sauvignon vineyard—he had made wine from that vineyard while he was at BV.

And so the deal was done. The company agreed to pay $14.5 million for the property to the William A. Hewitt Trust.

The Hewitt Ranch is surrounded by vineyards that make some of the best-known Cabernet Sauvignons in California, such as Beaulieu's Georges de Latour Private Reserve, Freemark Abbey's Cabernet Bosché and Niebaum-Coppola's Rubicon.

"This is a once-in-a-lifetime opportunity for us to purchase a vineyard of this distinction," Tom said in the announcement for the purchase. "This vineyard has produced some of the finest Cabernet in the Napa Valley."

Plans are now underway to develop a new brand featuring a single-vineyard Cabernet Sauvignon with an initial release of 3,000 cases in 2004. The vineyard is anticipated to ultimately produce up to 20,000 cases of ultra-premium quality wines.

As the company continued to expand its horizons, Tom Selfridge announced another acquisition in early April 2000. The company purchased the brand and inventory of Jade Mountain, a 7,000-case producer of Rhône-style wines, from its owner Jim Paras for $3.5 million. Chalone has a track record with Jim Paras and Jade Mountain – Paras is a friend of Phil Woodward's and the company has sold the Jade Mountain wines for several years. For Tom the acquistion made perfect sense: "This fits perfectly into our portfolio of wines because it has a niche all its own."

As the company embarks on its new mission to be the quality leader in wines made from many varieties, it takes with it the same passion for excellence its founders, Richard Graff and Phil Woodward, brought to bear on classic Burgundian varieties at Chalone Vineyard. It also takes with it a new leader in Tom Selfridge.

The baton has been passed and the next leg of the journey is well underway.

PART FOUR

❧

Embracing the Future

20 | *Our Philosophy: What We Believe as a Company*

RICHARD GRAFF AND PHIL WOODWARD STARTED CHALONE 30 years ago with an idea that there were people who really cared about high-quality wines. They didn't know how many were out there, but they could see a strong base of consumers who were drinking a lot of French wines. They knew that California wines belonged on the tables of those consumers as well. They set out to create wines that would excite those consumers just as Phil and Dick's first taste of the wines from Burgundy excited them.

Thirty years is a long time for any company to survive and thrive—especially one in a business as volatile and unpredictable as wine. There aren't too many wine companies in California that can honestly say that they have been in business for 30 years.

"You can count them, I suppose, on a couple hands," Phil said. "First, I think it's a huge milestone just to make it that far. Even more gratifying is that we have made it this far and we still have the integrity and vision of the company that we started. We're still in the high-end quality niche; we're still owned by people who care a lot about fine wines. And we're still run by people who have a passion for doing what we do. Even though a lot of the original people are gone, especially Dick, I have no doubt that the vision and passion will continue with Tom Selfridge at the helm. He's just as passionate as anybody has ever been about this company."

Passion is perhaps an overused concept in business generally. It certainly is part of every wine marketer's lexicon. But having real passion for what you do is a rare and wonderful thing. Passion is doing something because you love doing it. Passion is doing something that may not make sense financially, but it feels right in your heart. Passion is pretty much always doing things the hard way. Passion is almost always the opposite of expedience. Wine is about passion. And from day one Chalone has been about passion.

People respect that Chalone has been in business for a long time. There's a solidness, a permanence about the company that people in the wine business respect. That feeling of permanence was one of the key things that attracted Les Domaines Barons de Rothschild (Lafite) to the company in the first place. Their investment and their support over the 10 years they have been with the company is a statement that they share the core values and the mission of the company.

And that mission has remained the same since Phil and Dick joined forces on the benchland in 1972:

We grow by staying small.

"The strategy and the mission are still the same. Even today, we still grow by staying small," Phil said. "We add vineyards and wineries, none of which dominate the portfolio. I mean, we still run the company in the same manner by having common executive, administrative, financial, sales and marketing management but separate winegrowing and production at each winery. This allows us to make decisions at the lowest possible level and to focus on the quality of the wines."

We also grow by staying in touch with our community and being a responsible and generous member of that community.

The Chalone Wine Foundation is the company's program of outreach and support for the various communities in which the company's employees live and work.

"The Foundation was an idea that I had before Dick died," Phil said.

188

"I felt that as we got past our 25th year, I wanted to create a foundation that would somehow give back to those who have helped us get to where we are. It was really only an idea kicking around in my head until about three years ago. Then it dawned on me that maybe the best way to get started was to use the foundation as a vehicle to donate wine to non-profit organizations that use wine for fund-raising purposes. So we formed the Chalone Wine Foundation in 1997 with the idea of its being the vehicle that would give a budgeted amount of wine away to non-profit organizations for their fund-raising efforts. Today, we give away about $50,000 worth of wine per year.

"After Dick's death, I came up with the idea for a Richard H. Graff Scholarship Fund, with the money to be given to people who want to continue their education in food or wine, or both. We've done that a number of ways so far, and it's growing. The first one we did was a partnership with the American Institute of Wine & Food, of which Dick was a co-founder. We have a program with them in which each one of their 30 chapters across the United States can receive at least $1,000 a year from us for a legitimate scholarship in wine and food education. It must be used under the name of Chalone Wine Foundation/Richard H. Graff Scholarship Fund. We awarded 10 scholarships in 1998-1999 and expect to do another 15 in 1999-2000. We're also doing the same kind of thing at the Culinary Institute of America at Greystone. They're going to be in both wine and food courses. We're also funding scholarships with the California Culinary Academy in San Francisco, and with the Marin Educational Foundation.

"The third part of the foundation is what I call the Community Endowment Fund. I wanted to do something to give back to the communities where we have a winery, or in Napa's case, our headquarters. This fund is a little tougher to raise money for and it's a little bit tougher to find out exactly how to spend that money. For example, right now in Napa we're working with the Napa Valley Community Foundation, the County of Napa and the Culinary Institute at Greystone with a $10,000 grant to develop a program that would fund training and job opportunities for people in Napa who want to work in restaurants. It's more of an outreach program than anything else. The first class started in February 2000."

Phil sees the demand for scholarships like these, and the foundation's desire to grant them, growing substantially in the coming years. Where does the money come from to fund the scholarships? From a variety of sources, including individual cash and stock donations, proceeds from shareholder wine trips, the live auction at the annual shareholder celebrations as well as silent auctions at various shareholder functions throughout the year. In addition, profits from the sale of the Graff Family Vineyards wines also go to the foundation, as do profits from the sale of this book. Funding for the foundation reached over $500,000 by the end of its second fiscal year.

Phil would like to see much more money raised, and many more scholarships and grants awarded to deserving people. That's his mission for now, and he'll work with the same passion and drive to achieve that goal that he and Dick Graff brought to bear when they teamed up to build Chalone Vineyard nearly 30 years ago.

21 | *Our Shareholders:*
The Most Valuable Asset

WHY IS THE CHALONE WINE GROUP a public company?

The most important reason is not about the stock price, raising money or price-to-earnings ratios. It's not about market timing, bulls or bears—or any other animal, for that matter.

It's about the relationship Chalone has with the 12,000 or so people who have chosen to become shareholders in and therefore owners of the company. It's about their choice to invest in a company for reasons other than simple financial gain.

"One of the best things we can hope for is that our shareholders invest in us because they believe in us and believe in our wines," Phil said. "If they believe in us enough that they are willing to become an owner of the company, then we believe that they become the company's most powerful brand ambassadors. We spend a tremendous amount of time and effort to enhance this feeling of ownership through our shareholder relations program—from trips to dinners to the wine dividend credit, it's all done to enhance and build upon the connection a shareholder feels to the company. It's really not about our stock price—the truth is, it doesn't change much. It's about making our ambassadors, our shareholders, feel as connected to the company and to the wines as we possibly can."

Among the most public—and popular—benefits of being a shareholder in Chalone are the annual shareholder celebrations. These day-long events are part of a long tradition of friendship and community begun in the very earliest days of Phil Woodward and Dick Graff's involvement with Chalone. That inclusive attitude toward shareholders has continued, and today's shareholder celebrations are still true to the spirit conveyed by this invitation included as the closing paragraph in the 1976 Chalone annual report:

"We look forward to seeing you at the Annual Meeting on the 19th of June. As last year, the meeting will be conducted on the crushing platform of the new winery, and we will then adjourn to the MacWood A-Frame for an informal buffet. We had a very enjoyable time at last year's meeting, and hope even more of you will be able to come this year."

The tradition of holding the annual meeting and what has developed into the shareholder celebration on the property at Chalone Vineyard goes back to a time long before Chalone became a public company.

"We started doing the meeting at Chalone Vineyard, followed by some wine and something to eat. The first one was held in 1972. There couldn't have been more than 10 or 12 people there, and we had it at the cottage where Dick lived. We just sat around the room and talked a little bit about how the year was, opened some wine, had some bread and cheese, and that was it," Phil said.

"Then when my brother-in-law, Mac McQuown, and I built the 'A-frame,' we moved the meeting over there. As we added shareholders, maybe 30 or 40 people, we had it catered. We knew some people who had the guts enough to come all the way out there where there was no electricity or anything and actually prepare a meal for us. It would be a barbecue of some kind. And then as we got bigger we started to hold the meetings at the other wineries that we were acquiring. I remember at least three at Edna Valley. We had it both at the winery and at the Nivens' personal home. Then when we bought Carmenet, we had one or two there. The same with Acacia. In fact, the first year we had it at Acacia, which was the year we bought the winery [1986], was also the first year we had 500 people attending. That was just too much. That's when we moved it back down to Chalone and put it at our new home—the Pinnacles House, which we built after the A-frame burned. We had some tents put up and we could handle up to about 700 people there. But even then it started getting out of hand. That's when we moved it to where it is today, nearer to the winery. We've had as many as 2,000 people, but we try to limit it to closer to 1,500."

The annual shareholder celebrations are so popular and have become such social events for shareholders that it was becoming difficult to conduct the required business meeting. "It seemed that when you pass 200 people, they could care less about the business meeting," Phil said. "They didn't want to vote, they didn't want to take the time. It was kind of a struggle to get through that part because everybody was just waiting to have wine and food and enjoy meeting other people."

Phil and Dick made a decision to separate the business meeting from the shareholder celebration. They started holding the annual business meeting in the Bank of America auditorium in San Francisco and turning the shareholder celebration into an annual party sponsored by the wineries. And they began to charge admission to the celebration. Both Dick and Phil were a little worried that when they started charging admission no one would come.

"We were wrong," Phil said. "It didn't make any difference at all because we started selling wine and T-shirts, and then you could see that people really cared about having a good time. We typically will sell $300,000 worth of wine that day. I mean, it's amazing and incredibly gratifying—people just line up."

The annual shareholder celebrations are incredible logistical achievements. Coordinating all of the arrangements, invitations, and the on-site event itself is a major project for Kathryn Brinkmann, Chalone's head of special events, who works with a lot of people inside and out of the company to pull each event off.

And while the company does charge admission to each celebration, it's well worth the price for the fabulous food, great wine and camaraderie that comes from being part of a special family.

For years at the annual celebrations, Phil has entertained the shareholders with his tally of annual meeting attendance for major companies around the country.

"I don't know when I started doing this, but it had to be at least 15 years ago when we were consistently getting 500 or more people coming," Phil said. "It was interesting to me to look at how our attendance stacked up against the annual meetings of major public companies. Now, granted, our celebrations are not annual meetings per se, but I thought it would make a fun comparison. So I started calling some of these major companies like General Motors, IBM and AT&T and asking them how many people attended. We were really surprised at how very few people attend the meetings of those huge companies. We consistently drew more to our meeting. But being sort of a fan of Ben & Jerry's, too, because they went public about the same time we did with somewhat the same philosophy, I added them to the list as well, and made a joke that so many of their attendees are under 10 years old and that was why they had more attendees than we did."

22 | *Our People: Contributors to Both our Vision and our Success*

CHALONE PEOPLE BELIEVE THAT WE GROW BY STAYING SMALL. They believe that there's strength in numbers and that's why we don't let one brand dominate our company. We have multiple brands, each committed to quality and to the concept of place. Chalone people have a respect for the history of the company and a passion for quality and excellence.

The company has had many special people involved in its evolution—many of whom are still working there. Phil feels grateful to have had the opportunity to work with all of the Chalone people over the years and feels like they have all been part of a big family.

Phil shares his recollections of some of those special people below:

Conger Fawcett

"You might say that Chalone would not have been if it hadn't been for Conger Fawcett, who did all the legal work so that Estelle Graff (Dick's mother) could buy the original Chalone parcel. In the beginning years, Conger was the only person that had any kind of legal experience, so he kept us on the straight and narrow about how to do many things correctly and legally. Conger was always available. He was a very key player, and a very important part of the team. Today he's my brother-in-law, having married my wife's sister, and he still helps us but is no longer the company's full-time attorney."

Jack Chambers

"Jack Chambers was there before me because he had met Dick through Darrell Corti. Jack had a company called the Gavilan Import Company, and he was using one of our licenses to import wines for Darrell. Upon my arrival, he formed his own company, Chambers & Chambers, which we used for many years to broker our wines in Northern California. We eventually got to the point where it didn't make sense for them to handle our wines in California, but they still do in Hawaii. Jack was on the board for many years until the conflict of interest became too much."

John McQuown

"John McQuown, known as 'Mac,' is my brother-in-law, and I give Mac the credit for introducing me to wine. We spent hours upon hours talking about how we could make a business out of wine. Without his encouragement and without his knowledge, I probably wouldn't have done this. He was instrumental in getting this company off the ground. Not only did he help me make the decision to join in the first place, but he also helped me raise money. Mac was always and still is a stickler for quality and always pushed that side of the business. He knows a lot about wine, and he knows a lot about businesses. He was a great board member because he always played the devil's advocate; he always came up with something we hadn't thought of. He was with us for more than 20 years as a board member."

The Niven Family

"All of the Niven family, but especially Jack Niven, are very special to us because they had the faith in Dick and me early on when we really needed a partner to help us expand our company. The owners of Paragon Vineyards in San Luis Obispo, they decided to cast their grapes with us to form Edna Valley Vineyard. We've had our disagreements on everything from prices of grapes to personnel at Edna Valley, but they've always been supportive and they've always been involved. Today, the family's vineyard business is run by Jack's sons, John and Jim, and Jim is a member of the Chalone board."

Bill Hambrecht

"The more I look back at the story of our company, the more I realize how important a role Bill Hambrecht played. Today, of course, he's involved in a lot of different wine ventures. He has his own winery now, and he also has his family working for him in the wine business. Bill invested in us very early on and I felt that he was always a supporter in our growth. We would never have gone public without him. We got a hell a lot of credibility because of him. I'll always have a tremendous amount of respect for Bill for what he did for us, and who he is as a person. I think he's an incredible man."

Richard Kramlich

"Dick is a friend of Mac McQuown's. They both went to Northwestern University together, and hooked up again in California. Dick has always been in the venture capital business; he worked for Arthur Rock when he got out of Harvard and then opened his own firm, New Enterprise Associates, which has been one of the more successful venture capital firms in the country. But he also likes wine and was one of the original investors in Carmenet with Mac. I asked Dick if he would join the board and take Bill Hambrecht's place. Dick likes the relationship with us and we like the relationship with him. He's a no-nonsense board member and has been a great advisor to us especially in the fields of acquisitions, financing and personnel."

Baron Eric de Rothschild

"Eric de Rothschild has a great attitude and vision for Chalone that really matches up with ours. For him it's all about land. When you have a perspective that goes back four or five generations like he does, ownership of land and vineyards becomes really the bottom line. Winemakers come and go, equipment changes, but the land is still the same and the vineyards are still there. When you visit Château Lafite Rothschild and you see the vineyards, there's living proof that his philosophy is a good one."

Christophe Salin

"Christophe Salin, as president of Les Domaines Barons de

Rothschild (Lafite), has never missed a board meeting in 10 years. He's very much involved in the very top end of our company, from personnel decisions to top strategy. He has really embraced the way we do things in this country and understands how it works in terms of marketing and distribution. When I was CEO, I talked to him a lot and Tom does the same, so we're lucky to have him as DBR's primary representative."

Richard Hojel

Richard was the patriarch of the Hojel Family from Mexico City that became significant investors in Chalone. But Richard was more than a financial partner. A passionate and courageous man, he had people skills that allowed him to become Chalone's respected leader of the executive committee, and a great advisor to me. He entered and, upon his death in 1995, left our company much too quickly.

Jim Sullivan

Jim Sullivan, who still works for Hambrecht & Quist in New York was the person who went on the road show with me when we took the company public. We were the smallest company Hambrecht & Quist had ever taken public, and the fact that they could put someone like Jim on the account was incredible. We flew all over Europe and the United States and did all kinds of events. He'd never done anything quite like it. He was instrumental in helping us actually sell the shares to investors. We've continued to be friends and he's very, very successful with H&Q now. I'll always remember everything he did for us."

Wendy Bentson

"Wendy is my sister and when she graduated from the University of California at Berkeley in 1973, I asked her to help us out in our new offices in the basement of 655 Sutter Street in San Francisco by being our bookkeeper. Twenty-three years later, she left Chalone as its controller to take a similar position with a law firm in San Francisco where she lives. Her contribution to Chalone's success goes well beyond her accounting and financial talents."

William Hamilton

"I'd known Bill Hamilton from my days at Touche Ross in San

Francisco. Bill and I had been friends, and we stayed in touch after we both left accounting. So I offered Bill the opportunity to come and work for us and be our CFO in 1985, and it was something he really wanted to do. It brought him back to the San Francisco area and also give him a chance to be an entrepreneur with me. He was part of the team when we really grew the company from a fledgling million and a half dollars in sales to something close to $40 million by the time he retired in 1998."

Larry Brooks

"Larry Brooks was a key and important part of Chalone for many years. He made excellent wine at Acacia for more than 15 years and then really stepped up when I needed him to replace Dick Graff as head of all wine production for the company. Larry is currently a consultant to the company and is responsible for all the Echelon wines."

Michael Michaud

"Mike was around for more than 17 years, and was a key person in the production of wine at Chalone Vineyard. Prior to that, Dick and his brothers had always made the wines. When Dick began to lose interest in wine production, he turned it over to Mike. Mike was solely responsible for the wines for probably eight years or so. His last two vintages— the 1996s and 1997s—were some of the best wines we've ever made. Mike left to make wine under his own name from his vineyards on the Chalone benchland."

Mike Richmond

"Mike is the general manager of Acacia—his business card says 'The Prime Minister,' which tells you something about him. Mike is one of those invaluable people who is a true jack-of-all-trades in this business— from production, to sales, to marketing, to people skills. He can do it all. He does it a little bit differently, but he can do it all. He makes wine fun. He and I are right on the same wavelength. This is a fun business and you've got to keep it that way. He made it that way at Carmenet and now he's making it that way again at Acacia. He and his hospitality manager, whose title is 'Director of Euphoria,' make Acacia really hum. Mike goes back to Freemark Abbey in the late 1960s. There aren't very many guys like Mike Richmond left in this business. I have a lot of respect for him; he's a great guy."

Robert Farver

"I hired Robert Farver when he was with our distributor in Washington, D.C. I asked him to join the company as our eastern regional sales manager, which meant he was responsible for everything east of the Mississippi. He later became vice president of sales and distribution. Both Tom Selfridge and I have a great respect for him and for the team he's built and the way he can sell high-end wines. He's got an incredible work ethic and devotion to this company."

Tom Selfridge

"I was damn lucky to find somebody like Tom to take over the day-to-day management of the company because of his experience, because of his good people skills, and because of his feeling for the history and culture of this company. Tom and I get along extremely well. I couldn't have asked for anybody better than him to lead the company and keep the philosophy of growing by staying small. I think he's the right person at the right time to take this company to the next level—say, $100 million in sales."

23 | *Richard Graff:*
My Partner on the Wine Frontier

THIS BOOK WOULD NOT BE COMPLETE without recognizing the one man without whom none of this journey would have been possible. That man is Richard Graff.

This chapter is from Phil Woodward to everyone who knew Dick, everyone whose life was touched by this special man.

First of all, Dick was an extremely honest, ethical, moral person—so when I thought I might devote my future business life to having him as my partner, I felt that I had the right person. For all the 26 years we were together, that was always the case. That never, never changed. I knew almost from the very beginning that our social lives were completely different; and I felt it was a good thing because when you're building a business together, you really can't have your social lives together.

Dick's interests in the beginning, I thought, were totally wine and grapes—because that's all we ever talked about and that's all I ever saw him doing. Well, I was wrong. I'll never forget one of the things he told me early on, probably 1974 or 1975, when we were raising money and setting priorities for the business going forward. He said, "Don't think that I'm going to be living down at the vineyard all the time." That's when I first realized that Dick had many other interests. He was always a great reader, a great thinker, and he loved to write. Later on in his life, he wrote a couple of books that were interesting in a Dick Graff kind of way—intellectual and a bit esoteric. The first, "The Technique of Consensus," is about how people come together to make decisions. The second, "A Vision for the Millennium," describes Dick's view of the world and how to make it a better place.

He also began to show me that he had a great interest in cooking, as great as making wine. It didn't take me long to realize that he was a really good cook. Dick and Julia Child got to know each other through some of the early founding years of the American Institute of Wine & Food, and one time Julia came to visit Chalone and Dick cooked for her. I don't know how many people would have enough guts to cook for Julia Child. But Julia and her husband came, and Dick fixed chess pie from one of her cookbooks. She told Dick that it had never been prepared better. Dick was versatile—he could make a perfect omelet or roast a chicken and dazzle Julia Child at the same time.

I also began to realize that food was very much a part of his interests. He liked to grow herbs and had a garden and orchard at Chalone, which got me interested in it because I had done that earlier in my life back in Illinois. Of course, that interest really came to the forefront when he signed on as one of the co-founders of the American Institute of Wine & Food, along with Julia Child and Robert Mondavi. Dick continued that interest throughout his life, and at one point it caused a rift between the two of us—and the rest of the board—because it began to interfere with his work at Chalone.

When you saw some of the other things he did with his time, including writing and getting into philosophical issues on subjects like the World Forum, it was obvious that Dick was more than just a wine man. He was even more than a food and wine man. He was what many people would call a "Renaissance man" because he really did know a lot about the arts and literature and subjects that didn't have anything to do with winegrowing. He didn't have the money to do much about those other interests, but he always seemed to find a way to get other people involved who did have money to accomplish some of his dreams. Dick was a complicated guy to understand because he didn't sit down and tell you all of his personal interests. He wouldn't sit down and talk much about some of his desires. He just went out and did them.

⁓

CLEARLY, ONE OF DICK'S STRENGTHS was that he was a very charming man, a very persuasive man and a very intelligent man. Whatever the subject was, he was really passionate about it. And he could get you involved in it, and a lot of people got interested in what he had to say or do because of that. He could be classified as something of a leader in the initial stages of projects—at some point he would lose interest, and your leader was gone, off doing something new. He would admit this to me. He'd say, "You know, I get really excited about something, and I get people involved; then I like to move on and do other things." But when Dick was focused, he was really focused.

He was really focused on getting the American Institute of Wine & Food up and going, and for many years he was really the only one of the three founders who spent any real time at it. But for all his desire, he wasn't able to take that past the initial formation stages and make it viable financially.

⁓

AS I LOOK BACK, MY FONDEST MEMORIES OF DICK came from the first 15 years of the 25 years we worked together, because it was essentially just the two of us and a few other people.

I knew almost nothing about winemaking and grape growing. The times we would spend together at Chalone Vineyard in the little cottage on the property where he stayed, sitting around his table and just going over and over and over all of the things we wanted to do, the things that we needed to get done—those were the most memorable times I had. I'd bring my list, and we'd go over everything. We were working very, very closely together during those times. We would talk about when we were going to release a wine; we would talk about how he felt certain barrels ought to be used and when we ought to pick the grapes. I learned from that. And he would learn from me about how we needed to distribute the wines, or how much money we needed to raise and how we ought to spend it. We always talked about whom we were going to hire, no matter what the job was.

I would drive down on the weekend and stay in the A-frame—that was my job even though I had four young children at home. I did a lot of driving back and forth between Chalone and the Bay Area. Dick would be there, and we would spend half a day together just sitting and talking. No matter how hot it was down there or how cold it was in the winter, those were the best years.

Once we got into a formal office situation we never really had much contact there, because he just came in; he blew in and blew out. We rarely did promotional things together. We just couldn't afford to have two of us at the same event at the same time. So when we weren't talking about the business strategy in the beginning years, we were totally in our own respective jobs and worlds.

In the early days—up until about 1983—there wasn't a phone at Chalone. There wasn't any way to communicate other than in person or by letter. It was really tough to communicate. All of a sudden he'd appear in the San Francisco office. I'd say, "You're not supposed to be here; you're supposed to be at Chalone." But because there wasn't any phone, the only time we would talk was when I went to Chalone or he came to the City.

I got used to that after a while, because when he did pull his weight, he really did a great job. For instance, when we built the winery at Chalone, he did all the plumbing, he did all the electrical work and helped a lot on the air conditioning work. But then he'd take off for a week and you never knew where he was. I wanted to get the thing done.

I couldn't blame him, I guess—it was hard work. But you got used to it because Dick was that way. On the other hand, you had to admire him, because—well, we didn't have any money in the beginning years, and while I took a huge financial sacrifice, I felt I could do that for five years—he never complained about how little money he made in those years. To have a partner like that, who's not concerned about his personal compensation is rare. When you're building a company from nothing, and have two people who could agree to do that for five years or so, that was a lot. I have a huge amount of respect for him for that. He never asked for any more money unless I said we could spend it.

The other thing that I'll always remember is the annual shareholder celebrations. They were the greatest—even though Dick talked too long and told corny jokes. The fact was that for the 25 or so years we did it together, we would really put on a show. We really wanted to tell him, "You know, cut it. That was too much." It didn't make any difference to Dick; he just kept talking. In the early years the show went too long, but we did them year after year. I'll never forget those; they were great times.

Dick's legacy—his impact on California wine—really is the use of French oak barrels in the making of Chardonnay and Pinot Noir. There were French oak barrels being used in the making of Cabernet, but I think that even though he wasn't the first one, he was really the one who began to import them and use them consistently year after year for Chardonnay and Pinot Noir. He not only fermented the Chardonnay in French oak, he aged both the Chardonnay and Pinot in them as well. Hanzell was probably the first, but Dick was the one that really put it in general use and pushed it to become the standard way of making high-end Chardonnay and Pinot Noir. I really think he was the original Burgundian in California.

THERE'S NO QUESTION THAT I MISS HIM, because we were together for so long. We never really had any real battles. We had disagreements, but to the end we had a lot of mutual respect for one another.

As I moved out of the day-to-day management of the company, I started to think that it would be great to work with Dick again. I missed working with him on the small scale the way we started. There were some things that I wanted to do through the Chalone Wine Foundation that I thought Dick and I could do together again—come full circle.

I told him so. I'll never forget it. We had our last lunch together with a mutual friend at Bistro Don Giovanni in Napa. I told him that, through the foundation, maybe he and I could do some things together again—like we had done in the early years where it was just the two of us. I truly believed, and still do, that even after all the water that had flowed under the bridge, we would still be great at that. But the timing wasn't right. And then it was too late.

When I established the Richard H. Graff Scholarship Fund, I started to think of ongoing ways to raise the money to fund the scholarships. I had an idea that really made me feel great. We could come full circle again and make some of the specialty wines that Dick liked so well, do them in the old way, from vineyards that were his and his brothers' up on the Chalone benchland. We could make that wine, sell it and help fund the scholarships that way. So I came up with the name of "Graff Family Vineyards," which everyone seemed to think was appropriate. We decided to use one of Dick's favorite labels—the original Edna Valley label—that has now been changed to say Graff Family Vineyards.

We're making four wines. One was inspired by a wine Dick made—it was made by Chalone Vineyard under Dick's supervision. He called the wine "Vin Gris" in the true Provençal manner of using Mourvèdre and making it essentially from free-run juice. I remember Dick and I talking about the name Vin Gris and neither one of us really liked it because it was a French name, and we really wanted an English name. So I came up with the name—Mourvèdre Free Run. It's in the bottle, and we're selling it. It's getting a great reception. We made 150 cases.

We're also making the Muscat that Dick planted, called July Muscat.

It's a pretty obscure Muscat variety and I haven't found much information on it, but he got it from Wente, and they say that's what it is. It's really nice. I put it up in half bottles in very small quantities.

We're making a little of the Pinot Blanc, which is a bit different in style than Chalone is making now; there's much more oak on it, and it comes from some of the Pinot Blanc that Dick planted in his vineyard as well as some from his brothers' vineyard. Finally, we're making a Rhône blend called "Consensus," which is named after one of Dick's books—"The Technique of Consensus," which is about how people come together and make decisions. This is a coming together of Syrah, Mourvèdre and a little Viognier.

You put all four of these wines together and you have maybe 1,000 cases. The profits from the sale of these wines go to the Richard H. Graff Scholarship Fund. It's a fun thing to do. I enjoy it, and it's a good way of keeping Dick's memory alive. In many ways, a lot of people out there still remember him and will buy it because his name is on it and the profits benefit his scholarship fund. We sell it to shareholders through the catalog. I also have a broker in San Francisco, named Jay Freeman, who sells mainly to restaurants.

THERE WERE SO MANY THINGS ABOUT DICK AND ME that were different—but those differences never, never got in the way of our friendship or of our building the company. He had a great relationship with my wife; he had a great relationship with everybody else that was associated with the company, including the board members. We were the ultimate "odd couple" that made it work.

As I look back over the years, I find our business relationship to be special. Businesses don't get started, and partners don't stay together as we did. Today, in this industry, if a winemaker who may or may not be a partner becomes a star, he wants to go out on his own—and rightly so,

I suppose, but partnerships in the wine industry just don't seem to last. Even families can't stay together; it's tough. So I think one of the most remarkable things about Chalone is how well Dick and I did work together so long and stayed together for as long as we did. Both of us, in our own ways, established this company as something that can truly live on forever. And for that, and everything else, I thank Dick now.

Our journey has been one of breaking new ground, of successes and failures, but always fun.

To be continued....

Notes

Chapter 1

[1] Malcolm Margolin, The Ohlone Way: Indian Life in the San Francisco-Monterey Bay Area (Berkeley, CA: Heyday Books, 1978), p. 1.

[2] Ibid., p. 3.

[3] Ibid., p. 2.

[4] Ibid., p. 29.

[5] Ibid., p. 160–162.

[6] J.M. Gunn, ed., History and Biographical Record of Monterey and Benito Counties (Los Angeles Historical Record Co., 1910), p. 263.

[7] Fr. Zephyrin Engelhardt, Mission Nuestra Senora de la Soledad (unpublished, 1929), p. 40.

[8] Ibid., p. 42.

[9] Ibid., p. 45.

[10] Col. Agoston Harazsthy, Report on Grapes and Wine of California, from Transactions of the California State Agricultural Society (unpublished, 1858), p. 312–313.

[11] Leon D. Adams, The Wines of America, Fourth Edition (New York: McGraw-Hill Publishing Co., 1990), p. 194.

[12] J.M. Gunn, ed., History and Biographical Record of Monterey and San Benito Counties, p. 281.

[13] Langley's San Francisco Directories, 1880–1953.

[14] Soledad (CA) Bee, February 10, 1950.

Chapter 2

[15] J.M. Gunn, ed., History and Biographical Record of Monterey and Benito Counties (Los Angeles Historical Record Co., 1910), p. 314.

[16] Soledad Bee, October 11, 1929, p. 1.

[17] Salinas (CA) Daily Journal 1915 Progress Edition, unpublished.

[18] The Rustler, Salinas Valley, 1915, p. 43.

[19] Ibid.

Index

The Chalone Wine Foundation is the scholarship and community outreach arm of the Chalone Wine Group. Established in 1997, the foundation is charged with three primary missions. First, it donates wine to selected non-profit organizations for their fund raising efforts. Second, it provides scholarships to fund students in their wine and food education. Several scholarship programs have been established with leading culinary schools. The third mission is one of community outreach in the various communities where the company has a presence. The foundation is funded through individual cash and stock donations, as well as the proceeds of company-sponsored shareholder events and auctions. All profits from the sale of this book also go to the foundation.